A TRUE STORY OF PRESCRIPTION MEDICATION

CRAIG DAWTREY

Polydrugged Into Insanity

© 2019 Craig Dawtrey All Rights Reserved

No part of this book may be reproduced or transmitted in any form or by any means, electronic or mechanical, including photocopying, recording, or by any information storage and retrieval system, without permission in writing from the publisher.

This book is not intended to diagnose or prescribe any treatment for any medical or psychological condition(s), nor does it claim to prevent, diagnose, treat, mitigate or cure any medical or psychological conditions.

It contains the ideas and opinions of its author and is intended solely to provide helpful information on a number of subjects. It is sold with the understanding that the author and publisher are not engaged in rendering medical, health or any other kind of personal professional services in the book. The reader should consult his or her medical, health or other competent professional before adopting any of the suggestions in the book.

The author specifically disclaims all responsibility for any liability, loss or risk, personal or otherwise that is incurred as a consequence (directly or indirectly) of the use and application of any of the contents of this book.

ISBN 978-0-620-85511-2 (print)
Published: November 2019
Edit, Typeset, eBook and Cover by: www.typesettingbook.com

ABOUT THE AUTHOR

Fist time author Craig Dawtrey is South African born. A graduate of the University of the Witwatersrand and a passionate health and fitness advocate, Craig has accumulated two martial arts black belts and completed two South African iron man triathlons which set a foundation of goal-setting and self-discipline. He is the father of two adult children and has been involved in sales and marketing for over twenty years. A strong believer in the adage 'what doesn't kill you makes you stronger', he is a lover of nature and an enthusiastic communicator.

Contact Craig via:

dawts63@gmail.com
www.facebook.com/polydruggedintoinsanity

The car park of Helen Joseph Hospital in acute withdrawal

16 months later and weaned off all the medication

ACKNOWLEDGEMENTS

As always there are so many people involved in one's life and that tend to forge us. These are but a few of the ones that went beyond.

Firstly, I need to thank my daughter and son who had to share this horrendous journey with me, never giving up hope-against–hope for the breakthrough even when I had 'lost it'. My mother, Jean Dawtrey, for showing the most amazing love and resilience under very trying times that should be spared from one at this stage of her energetic and enthusiastic life. Her maternal instinct never falters. My sisters Paige Holmes and Kim Dawtrey for encouraging, fighting for, and talking to me and for me even when I could not. My dear friends Gavin Murphy, who dug deep at all times, and Brian Crossan for never giving up hope, even pretending to be my brother so he could visit me outside of 'visiting hours'.

Cindy James Delport and Shelby Geyer Anderson, two of my childhood friends who appeared out of nowhere and always spoke to me and the family. I would love to believe I would have done the same for you if the tables were turned.

Debbie Johnson Crooks my bubbly cousin for support and humour in my recovery.

Bridget Hilton-Barber for reading a very rough draft and replying that she "burst into tears" at the end. Your professional opinion encouraged me to complete the project.

To all the patients at Butterfly Lodge...even though it might not have appeared so at the time I shared your pain and bathed in your support, so thank you and I hope your healing happens soon.

Sonia, my Book Guru, for making the editing and finalisation of this book a breeze.

*This book is dedicated to my son and daughter
In you I see I did something right*

CONTENTS

1	*Introduction*
5	DARK AWAKENING
29	THE SEARCH FOR PERFECTION
62	ANOTHER DAY
88	RIVERSIDE CLINIC
24	THE KRUGERSDORP STAY
165	PUSHED TOO FAR
184	DEEP IN THE SYSTEM
225	BACK TO BUTTERFLY LODGE
239	TREADING WATER
256	THE BREAK THROUGH
273	THE LAST DAYS IN RECOVERY
280	*Conclusion;*
280	*On Medication And Psychiatric Drugs*
286	*What We Wish Family And Friends Knew About Psychiatric Medication Withdrawal*
289	*Psychiatric Medication Recovery Tips*
293	*On Marriage And Communication*
296	*On Living And Life*

INTRODUCTION

> Tell your story.
> Shout it. Write it.
> Whisper it if you have to.
> But tell it.
> Some won't understand it.
> Some will outright reject it.
> But many will
> Thank you for it.
> And then the most
> Magical thing will happen.
> One by one, voices will start
> Whispering "Me, too."
> And your tribe will gather.
> And you will never
> Feel alone again.
>
> —K.R. Knost

When I started writing this book, it was initially on the recommendation of various therapists. They proposed that writing my emotions would be a cathartic experience.

At the very time of being poly-drugged, I had lost the ability to write and talk and so, any of the experiences were temporarily locked away in my mind. The strangest thing was that I had mentally and visually recorded it moment-by-moment, I believe due to the continuous trauma that I had been exposed to.

It was only a few months after the conclusion of my stay at Butterfly Lodge that I recovered the will and ability to read and write. The process started as a bitter and angry retaliation against the people who had put me in that situation, and revenge was the single driving factor. As the story grew and the process was transferred from pen to paper, I realised that there was the possibility that it might assist other people going through depression or other mental trauma.

The realisation that there were a huge number of people either on psychotropic medication—or considering going on it, struggling to come off of it and unable to interpret what they were going through, the fear of the unknown consequences, or the withdrawal effects of the medicines they had been prescribed—caused me to rationalise that my experience and memory of it might be of help.

Online support groups made me realise that the large number of people out there in the world were talking about the same symptoms I had shown and felt, and that as a survivor of psychotropic medication, I could possibly give them hope for a way out of the mental hell they are living in.

I hope that in the reading of this book, the patient, parent, child, or support group of the sufferer may identify with emotions or behaviours that are being presented and not understood. My wish is that the doubters and naysayers find validity in the claims of the depression sufferers and, dare I say, 'victims' of iatrogenic illness, and at last say "I understand and believe you."

In order to protect my children and other characters in the book, I have changed certain names. Those names that are of other characters in the story that are actual names have been left as such with those individuals' permission.

Institution names have been changed as well.

I have tried to keep the story as human as possible so that it might differentiate from other scientific and medical journals; yet, I have included definitions in layman's terms in the hope that it will be easier understood.

Poems that appear intermittently were all written after the fact as well and came to me at different stages of the writing process.

DARK AWAKENING

I have shown no progress out of the mental darkness into which I have been forced.

My crossed legs, covered in state-sponsored clothing, signify the control that has been placed over me. The inappropriately smart black shoes that have spent all night on my feet leave a polish stain soiling the cheap white sheets they brush.

Dawn slowly creeps into the curtain-less, cold ward and slips in pink shadows that momentarily colour the bare white walls.

I rise gently so as not to awake the other patients; not so much to disturb their drug-induced sleep, but more to avoid the poisoned personalities that the drugs seek to cure.

The soft shoes shuffle across the vinyl floor and make their way to a small cabinet against the wall. A blue-faced wristwatch with a gold and silver strap folded neatly underneath it sits atop the cabinet. The watch hints at happier times where once a joyous life had lived. I place my hand on the shiny face and gently lift it from the cabinet. The hands have stopped their repetitive path around the face and tell only of the hour they had ceased.

I stare deeply into the face of the watch, urging the hands to move once again; to bring life and purpose to the glistening face. Yet, it stares stubbornly back at the emotionless eyes willing it on…Nothing.

The pink shadows that crawl across the wall and make it blush at its nakedness grow lighter and lighter, rendering the wall a sickly yellow first and once again a pale, stale white.

The dark, still beds in the ward start to gain life as the poisoned minds start to awaken. The blankets change form as they morph and give birth to living beings. The beings spill out of their temporary cotton cocoons as the call rings out, "MEDS TIME…MEDS TIME!"

Sadly, it is day once again.

A BEAUTIFUL ENDING

So much of life passes us by before we identify a period that influences us and changes us forever. That moment varies for everyone. Some people never have a defining point as they merely drift in oblivion through the ether. Their experience might be easy or it might be difficult. The difference is that some people are aware of it while others are not.

Life in its infancy finds us occupied with survival and dependence. We grow naturally through a physical and emotional instinct and process. For some, choices are made in advance and they work out as they or their parents planned for them; yet, others stray from the plan.

Many are swayed from their targets; be it by circumstances and external forces or once again, for some, by their own choices.

My wife, Jackie, and I had been married for twenty-seven years and had been courting for an additional three years before that. To us and the casual observer, the relationship had always been comfortable and if not perfect, then damn close to it. We had a two-year age gap between us and common friendships coupled with shared history, certainly made the prospects appear bright.

In our era and at the age of the mid-to-late twenties, people started becoming engaged and planned the life ahead. For many, this was after the completion of national military service. At the time, all young white males over the age of sixteen were conscripted to complete two years of national service. The fatal alternative was to become a conscientious objector and be jailed for three years or leave the country. The option of leaving the country was not available to many, as the travel options for a holder of a South African passport were severely limited because of Apartheid-era travel restrictions imposed on us by countries outside of South Africa. Accordingly, most of us had no option, and reluctantly completed the two years in the army, navy, air-force, or police force. My call-up was to the South African army.

Having completed the two years of national service, I joined the same university as my wife-to-be for a four-year course. She was in her third year of an undergraduate degree in the Arts, and was about to embark on a post-graduate diploma in teaching. I was about to start with a degree in sport science.

Having attended the same high school, I had known the 'love of my life' some ten years prior to this. I had, for many years, joked that "she had a major crush on me" which I had resisted for five years, and it was merely coincidental that we had managed to meet again and make a relationship of it. The reality was that the converse was true.

I had always remembered the pretty face of the smiling girl that I assumed would NEVER have LIKED me.

LIKE is such a big word in retrospect. In my opinion, it is WAY more meaningful than LOVE. One can always love someone, but to not like them is to reject the essence of who they are.

One can love a child, yet not like them by virtue of their behaviour or nature. The same would apply to a parent, sibling, or spouse, I guess.

I prefer to *like* someone.

FAST-FORWARD TO FEBRUARY 2015

We had been looking forward to the date as typically 'big' celebrations were separated by ten years.

This month was her fiftieth birthday and as such, a significant one.

Let us celebrate! Friends and family together. And so, we set the date for the evening of February 17, 2015.

Dress code: Broadway hit play, Chicago, read the invitation. A wonderful group of appropriately dressed friends, family, and acquaintances congregated for the party.

South Africa was experiencing an electrical power supply crisis at the time. Due to extremely poor management and institutional corruption in government, the national electricity supplier, Eskom, had been inclined to have both planned and unplanned supply cuts known as 'load-shedding'. It was highly unpredictable at the time, and it was wise to prepare for that negative eventuality and at the same time hope for the best. In our case, the electricity failed.

Just as the power supply was cut to the general area, the lights switched off and the background music stopped as the DJ sighed with resigned acceptance. A humorous cheer rose from the guests as they all realised what had just happened. We were, of course, prepared for this eventuality as I had organised a rental generator for back-up.

With the determination of a confident, empowered South African male I approached the generator with macho glee. Aggressively jerking the pull-start rope, it snapped, requiring me to then spend another hour with uncles and friends attempting to fix it. The contingency plan was failing. This didn't get us down at all as the men, fresh beers in hand, continued with the task. Eskom was presumably sorting out the electricity problem as we were frantically trying to fix the generator, if only for a few hours.

With this delay in the proceedings, we decided that the speeches should be moved to the front of the agenda as—of course—we were SO organised.

Eventualities anticipated and problems circumvented, we continued undeterred. After all, we were the 'perfect couple', weren't we?

Lisa, our daughter, and her friends performed a Poi fire show for the guests on the lawn. They swayed next to the swimming pool, with fire and cables swirling around their heads and bodies. Robert, our son, played the electric guitar as musical backing for the pyrotechnic show. The kids sure impressing all.

After all, we were the perfect family, weren't we?

After a few hours, the power was eventually restored and the party continued. No-one had left during our electrical hiatus and the drinks and friendly conversations kept everyone in a happy summer mood. The resumption of power brought the music back online and we all danced late into the evening as the DJ selected appropriate tunes from his massive list to accommodate the various generations attending. Drinks continued to flow as tasty plated food was provided by the caterers. Fun and happiness were had by all.

Once the evening had wound down (after a friendly call from the local police due to a noise complaint from a miserable neighbour) people started leaving for their short journeys home.

Compliments were showered upon us and we bathed happily in them. Adulations were accepted graciously as the guests left for home. Still elated and doing some late night tidying up, we basked in our glory. What a wonderful couple we were. Sigh!

This must have been the best party anyone could ever have thrown. Or so it felt to us.

We had entertained, mingled with, and pleased our guests according to the high standard we had always set for ourselves.

The rest of 2015 continued relatively smoothly. In retrospect, it is possible that we went into the next phase of the year expecting that our perfect lives would continue in this vein. I had no doubt that the marital relationship was in a good place and we would be good for years to come. We had toiled through SO much emotionally, and had even overcome some severe financial traumas over the past decades that I, certainly, felt we had conquered the world. The stresses had not broken us, but bonded us tighter into a very capable unit. The corner of defeat had been turned long ago and there lay only good days ahead of us.

We had MADE it. It was OUR time. It was OUR turn. Our family of four all celebrated birthdays during the first three months of the calendar year.

Mine fell on January 3rd, Jackie on February 17th,

Robert on March 11th, and finally Lisa, on March 18th. With the family's annual birthday blessings and other significant days past, we moved into the early-to-mid part of the year in joyful anticipation. Summer and then autumn, at this point, inclusively.

There was nothing to fear as hardship had forged us into a formidable family and couple. We felt that we could handle every challenge at this stage. Extended family from both sides of the marriage bonded us together. Between mine and Jackie's parents, they had amassed over a hundred years of happy marital lives combined, and I was sure we would follow, based on the good guidance and example they had set for us. It was, after all, a positive target to aim for.

We were all strong; Happy; Proud.

As months do, in our mid-to-latter years, they slipped by with hardly a beat. With our son in his final year of high school and our daughter graduating from university, I figured that this was the time we had both been waiting for. As a couple we could—and should—start escaping to romantic and interesting retreats monthly.

It was OUR TIME at last!

We had spent twenty-nine years in the process of building a family and a relationship to last. The photographs were there to prove it, and we had only to add to the albums of prosperity to confirm this.

Glory be to us!

___ ___ ___

I bow a deep, low bow as I enter the dojang.

"Ahn young ha sim nee kah, Kwan jung nim!" I boom out proudly as I humbly look at the shorter, stocky Korean man I revere so.

"Ahn young ha sim nee kah, Craig," echoes back from the far side of the temple hall. Bare-footed, I enter and stride confidently across to shake his powerful hand and bow once again.

As a sign of respect, I turn my back on him and wrap the broad black belt around my waist and fasten it in the required manner... one method ONLY, and both ends hanging parallel at the exact same length in front of my legs. Is the uniform neat?

Satisfied that it is, I complete a one-eighty degree turn and stride midway across the fighting mats where once again, another turn finds us facing each other, ready for training.

The Buddhist bells ring apologetically out of respect to the grand master and his student as we prepare to start the lesson—some of which must be repeated to achieve unattainable perfection. The balance is to be learnt as new skill and refined over time.

The mutual respect is palpable as we ease into the ritual beginning of an art founded centuries before our bare feet had pounded the ground and kicking bags. The same art handed down from master to student in the way of the empty hand and foot... human power tempered by a gentle heart and humble way. There is no place for tempers and vanities once we don the uniform. Respect commands respect here; it is an unspoken agreement.

Slow, defined stretches and powerful kicks thud as the impact of hardened, bare feet alternately pulverise muted bags. The echoes speak repeatedly.

WEEKENDS AWAY

The two of us had begun the year after the beautiful family birthdays by spending a weekend at a 'Boer and Brit' celebration in a rural dump of a village on the Highveld called 'Val'. On these dry and dusty grounds, we met great people, and very cold weather.

The area held a lot of history specifically related to the Anglo-Boer war and had visits from regular casual tourists that passed through on weekends. The locals had decided to place it on the social map by having a weekend commemorating the war happenings of the beginning of the twentieth century. People came for the festivities dressing the part, parading their period costumes in the main street.

Men in 'Red coats' from the British side, mixed with others representing the Boer contingent in their duller, but more appropriately earthy camouflage and khaki colours.

It was a bitterly cold weekend, however we stayed in the old local hotel and joined in as enthusiastically as anyone could.

We spent a cold night drinking and eating in the bar, humorously named the *Moeggeploegkroeg* (the 'tired of ploughing bar').

There were several very interesting monuments

to the fallen soldiers dotted around this area of the old Transvaal (now named Gauteng) and we tried to visit as many of them as we could find during the short weekend spent there. This fun and historically interesting weekend spurred us on to declare that we would spend at least one weekend every month on a retreat no more than two hours travel from home. Done deal.

Month two of the travel agreement entailed a trip off to Kwazulu-Natal as that was also a two-hour flight and drive, combined. This appealed to me, as I had managed to favourably manipulate the rule of being within two hours of our home to suit us both.

We enjoyed gentle time alone walking, chatting, eating, reading, and bonding as we eased into the new phase of life.

We were entering the 'golden years' of our lives, as I was reliably told by an aunt at my wife's fiftieth birthday party.

Month three of the arrangement overlapped with our twenty-sixth wedding anniversary, and found us on the beautiful Indian Ocean islands of the Seychelles. I had painstakingly researched the resort and the various islands in the chain to find the best place for our accommodation, excursions, and financial needs. I had settled on Paradise Beach Resort.

It had been built adjacent to a two-kilometre-long beach-front, which would suit our early morning walking plans as well as water deep enough to swim in at both low and high tide. I could snorkel close to shore, and there was a small village within walking distance for purchasing gifts and snacks. It was based on one of the smaller islands in the archipelago, named Praslin Island, where we would have ten days of sand, sunshine, and warmth that would split the South African winter in half.

I had always loved this method of travel to the tropics or to the northern hemisphere, for once we had returned from the islands, there would be but six weeks of cold weather back home whereupon our summer would relieve us from our version of winter, once again bathing us in our familiar African heat.

We laughed and danced at the hotel at night and then during the day, we swam amongst tropical fish. We walked to and on exotic beaches as the blissful ignorance of what was going on behind my back evaded me. Boat trips and island-hopping experiences belied a one-sided latent tension of which I was blissfully unaware. We had arrived at our new space in life in comfort.

Photos and memories were shared on social media with the unwitting arrogance that comes with this twenty-first century behaviour. We were unwittingly saying, "Everyone, look at us!"

As they say, pride comes before a fall!

For month four of our excursions, we found ourselves once again in the province of Kwazulu-Natal on the South African east coast. It is a subtropical region that is blessed with the Drakensberg mountain range and hundreds of kilometres of pristine coastline. I had received 'inside information' from a friend about a beautiful venue, and had decided to use this as a surprise for my wife. I approached it with suppressed excitement. Jackie had always had a deep love for the mountains and I knew this retreat would fit the profile perfectly. I had secretly booked the trip and told her to pack for a mixed experience, as I didn't know what the weather would be like.

"It's not a beach holiday, but a swimsuit could be useful." We were flying, but domestically. No passport required.

After a fifty-minute flight into King Shaka International airport, followed by a one-hour drive, we eased into the parking lot next to the reception area that looked over the Oribi Gorge. A magnificent sight greeted us as we peered over the railing and drew the fresh country air into our lungs.

This was a five-star boutique hotel and every executive suite was designed and built with a view. Romance was personified in magnificent vistas from elevated bedroom suites mounted precariously against the top face of the gorge and gift-wrapped in glass sheet panoramas. I glanced across at Jackie and beamed. Seeing the look of awe on her face as she looked at the view, I knew immediately I had made the correct decision. I had learnt to listen, absorb, consider, and then I had acted upon the emotional request from her.

The resident chef prepared gourmet meals in the small, private restaurant that had followed our long walks in the mountains. We cooled down with relaxing afternoon drinks at the rim-flow pool, which was also built with uninterrupted views of the Oribi Gorge until it flowed onward out to the mountains and plains beyond. It was a true romantic boutique hotel that satisfied all aspects that it had promised.

The September spring eased in and family life was back in full swing. There was a jaunty lift in the atmosphere and a promise of summer to come. Yet, with all the joyful jet-setting, October would be the month of the beginning of the end.

THE FAMILY CRUMBLES

Robert and I are sitting in the backyard enjoying the soothing kiss of the lovely, warm October sun. Jackie is just a short way off in the garden, engaged in thought.

The sadness was borne upon a message meant for illicit lovers carried from one mobile phone to another's.

My ears are assaulted with buzzing and a hum that I have never experienced before—like an electric wire that has been short-circuited. All peripheral noise is unceremoniously shoved aside and tunnel vision shrouds my eyes as a wave of confusion envelops me.

Her mobile phone stares blankly back with no empathy for what it is showing me. What is this thread of communication I see? One lousy song from her playlist—which generally had a nice mix, especially for a Sunday afternoon family lunch—had caused me to pick up her phone to change the song to a better one.

There it is! Surely, my wife's phone is lying to me!

"What is this shit?" I enquire incredulously, whilst

holding up the offending instrument.

"I wondered when you would find out," came her muted, sterile response.

You must be joking! "Find out what?" I ask.

This is becoming increasingly absurd... The love of my life, the one I had happily and willingly dedicated the last thirty years of my life to? This cannot be possible!

It is said that in the twenty-first century affairs are started in the chat-room and not in the bedroom. I find out to my detriment that this is so.

Tears of disbelief well up in my eyes as my head starts shaking uncontrollably, involuntarily conveying "No, this can't be!"

Despair and shock swirls into an emotional cocktail of anger that swamps my previously calm mind. My son looks on in confusion as I kick a garden chair over in anger; it tumbles over the patio, trimming a couple of rose bushes and settles untidily on the lawn.

"What's the matter, dad?" he asks, confused and shocked.

Jackie's eyes widen as she stands rooted to the ground. Like a deer, cornered.

She is speechless for a change, but not for the reasons I would ever have wished for. The shocked anger whirls through my head as I ask, "Who is this?"

An uncomfortable silence ensues.

The silence stalls, hanging in an elevated pause, as fearful breaths stay. Honest answers follow swiftly, and the lies do not like to be taunted from their hiding place.

Eventually, the awkward silence is broken.

"Mark," is the whispered answer offered.

"Mark, the bald guy with the grey beard who looks like a Hobbit from middle Earth?" I don't say it aloud, but that's what flashes through my head.

"Surely not?"

This married, so-called 'family' man that she is referring to, had been standing in my kitchen, talking to me and my children a few short weeks ago. I had welcomed him into my home. I had offered my key of friendship to the home and he had kept it—stolen it—and then later used it to break into my home to steal and disrupt the happy place I had spent thirty years building!

I had honestly believed her explanation a few weeks earlier that they were busy with a business project. I trusted her! I trusted him! Why would they do this?

Jackie and I had never had any serious arguments about anything. There was no emotional or physical abuse from either side. We were a happy couple; or so I thought. Doubt takes trust as her mistress as I shout out, "Phone him, phone him now!"

Jackie tries to avoid this uncharacteristic demand from me for a short while, and then reluctantly and awkwardly calls Mark on her phone from around the side of the house.

In anger and frustration, I follow her and say to her, "Give me the phone. I want to speak to the fucker!"

"No, Craig, leave it. I will handle it"

She refuses the demand and as the accommodating person I have always been, I hold back until their short conversation is finished.

"What did you tell him?" I snap.

"I told him that the relationship was inappropriate and that it had to stop," she unconvincingly replies.

Reluctantly believing her, I angrily storm from the front of the house and then immediately retreat through the kitchen and out the back door. On the way out, I punch the stable door off its hinges. I am angry—REALLY angry! What the hell is happening to my life?

Robert follows in my wake of confusion and anger. He is now aware of what is going on. What about the innocent ones? The children who are dragged into the sordid mess unwillingly, shattering their fairy-tale life for the selfish gains of adults. What about them?

It's my life and I will do what I like because "I deserve it"?

"It's MY turn," she says. Fuck the rest.

This was the beginning of the end of the marriage and stable family unit I had loved and enjoyed so much, although at the time, I don't know it. The experience is at this stage a nightmare from which I cannot awake.

The late afternoon and into the evening are split between moments of silence, tears, and angry discussions. Impassioned pleas are interspersed with moments alone and partnered whispers. What the hell has our wife and mother done? What has she done to me, to us—and ultimately to herself?

Later in the evening, whilst we all sit in the lounge, she shuffles in, sits down on the couch next to us and sighs, "I think I killed something today."

You don't fucken say goes through my mind, yet my tearful response is a forgiving, "No, not killed; but you certainly severely dented something today."

The spontaneous hug I offer her for mutual consolation is accompanied by tears running down my cheeks. I genuinely don't want any of us to be hurt. The hug is also a wrapping of protection and consolation. I honestly think that the situation can be fixed. After all, she did say it was a 'meeting of the minds' more than anything else.

Yes, sure. Whatever.

A swirling, hazy, numb night drags past slowly, unforgivingly and with no remorse for my desperately needed slumber. Occasionally, I drift into a spiral galaxy of darkness with the distant whispers of light hope from stars that snatch sadness for a brief glimmer in sleep. Intermittent breaks from disturbed slumber jerk me back from dreamy lies, shoving me into a new morbid reality. Sleep, as little as there is, teases me with promises of relief from the harshness of this new life and its brutal, cruel truths.

I find myself trying not to touch Jackie, resisting the temptation to hold her. This behaviour is alien to me. She is the person who had done this damage to me, so how am I supposed to react?

The questions race through my mind…
How does one embrace the abuser of your soul?
Who is this beside me?
Why hadn't I seen anything different?
Not recognised anything wrong?

No signs.
No sadness.
No anger.
No conflict.
No perceived dissatisfaction.

I made a desperate attempt at clinging to her body in the early morning as stuttered sleep breaks.

"Craig, did you have a nightmare?" Came her gentle retort.

"No," I whispered. "The nightmare starts whenever I wake up."

For the first time in my life, reality is worse than fiction. How do you cling to the loved one for sustenance and comfort when she is the one that has borne the agony upon you?

Who do you turn to for help when THE ONE is the one who has betrayed all you believed and trusted in? The wife, lover, best friend, confidante, and soul-mate bares the sword that pierces the veneer of trust and kills your love. Instantaneously.

Who do you turn to?

Confiding in another is to betray the betrayer. The significant other is changed into an insignificant other, yet that acceptance is at once a betrayal of your own faith and belief.

I love you, yet you have shown yourself to not love me, whatever you say to the contrary. I want SO to believe you, but your actions tell me otherwise. Please don't do this to me, yet you HAVE. Stop it. You can't reverse what has been started.

The momentum of sadness kicks in. It shoves you

down the hill and has no remorse as it snow-balls out of control.

Over the next days, I spend hours outside in quiet contemplation as the gentle, yet unforgiving breeze stirs a saddened carousel of faded leaves around my feet. Swirling, the leaves taunt my toes with a quiet tapping, and a hesitation. They tilt backward and stare up at me with their dry, cracked faces wondering what is wrong. As the breeze drops briefly away, they rest against my feet in sympathetic support.

As if the leaves are reminded that their time for mute comfort is over, they at once beat a rustling, hasty retreat as nature's breath picks up on its own haphazard nonchalance only to desert me in quiet contemplation once more.

Glimpsing a pearl of hope above a river of doubt, I write:

Dear Jackie

Taekwondo as a hobby or sport is very big in my life, but needs time to develop. I always said to you that I needed to get to the end of 2015 and get my master's qualification, so I could then make the change of focus to Hapkido and start to create a training business on the side with Eddie.

That year is now done, and I achieved the master's grade (ironically as I write this without you around it all seems meaningless).

Jackie, my love, change needs time and one can't make knee jerk reactions.

These changes only feel meaningful if you are there to share them with me. I will always only feel incomplete without you there.

But this is what spouses do. They have discussions about the day. Often, you just have to nod and empathize. We are not asking for a solution.

Firstly, why didn't you speak to me and the children about things that were bothering you early on instead of waiting until a potential marriage and family-destroying event? Surely you with all your knowledge, know that communication is critical?

I believe, Jackie, that one of the most overriding causes is that you live mostly inside your beautiful, intellectual mind.

Your introspection can be damaging as you ask the questions of us in your head, write it down in a diary that is only seen by you, and then you expect us to respond and make a change in our collective lives, and we have not even heard it from your mouth.

You have decades of journals piled up with interesting thoughts that think, plan, discuss issues and people…, but those very people—me, Lisa, and Robert—don't get to hear, see, or have the chance to respond to your thoughts... Just because you have written them down in a book does not make us hear them.

Talk to us please!?

If your mind is in the poems and diaries, then we need to see your mind and thoughts so that we can understand you better... You do so much of this, but don't actually share any of it with us... How do we know? If you feel that last year was the one that made the biggest difference, then let's look at the last three. This is purely for perspective. My dad's death was devastating for all of us, not just me. I took over two years to recover enough to speak about it. This nearly broke that side of the family. Now I feel it is sorted, we have a crisis much more important to me right at home.

You started your master's course, which lasted two years. Most of this time was spent in your office, away from us all. You'd pop down for supper and the family interaction lasted possibly an hour. This was meaningful time, but we accepted it for our beautiful family. You still do that often during your working year. We like you to join us...We love you to join us... We are a family when you come down and make it whole. I sometimes wonder whether you would have come down if I didn't insist on the 6:00 o'clock wine glass call...

You get so into your zone and head that I think you aren't aware of the impact downstairs. I can't imagine life without me making the wine call or unexpectedly bringing you a cup of tea.

You make us whole. What would life be for us with a dinner table for three? The thought breaks our hearts. Your weeks away at Stellenbosch were not easy, but we coped for you—happy wife, happy life.

The beautiful parts of the year...

We started cooking together as a family. Both you and I—the non-chefs—actually cooking?! And enjoying it... Good food, good wine, and bonding. Beautiful holidays and trips together. Regular trips; happy ones with no indication of pending problems with us... How hard was it to hide it so deeply?

Dinner dates together. Dinner with family. Dinner with the children. Going to rugby with Robert. Sundowners on the patio and tea upstairs... These are all good.

Love Craig

"Jackie, I think that I was possibly suffering from contented complacency," I apologise.

This is a compromise I offered to deflect some of

the blame away from her and thus appear complicit in the failure. What is 'contented complacency', exactly?

I think that over a thirty-year relationship, one becomes used to the relationship that one is in, and what it offers. Not in an intentionally negative way at all; we just follow routines and build rapport with each other and the family lifestyle. Complacency manifests in the sense that we are comfortable with the family dynamic. We feel safe there and proud of what we have become. We see no wrong in the relationship structure, as there appears to be no indications of trouble in paradise.

We settle back and enjoy the view. We bask in the comfortable life we have created for ourselves and make little effort to affect changes, for we deem them as being unnecessary. We adopt the 'Don't try and fix it if it is not broken' mentality.

Receiving a muted response from her about the letter, I am encouraged to continue to write and evaluate my thoughts.

The life coach is in action again!

"Good god!" I shout. "Give me something to work with here!"

I was fighting for my marriage and family's future!

THE SEARCH FOR PERFECTION

What is perfection?
It is but a perceived nirvana of idealism created by a philosophical mindset that settles upon the most suitable definition of what the group or person is searching for.
In the pursuit of perfection, the beauty of normality passes by, staring so far ahead allows the blinkers of the now to obscure the possibilities.
The future is not tangible yet the present is.
Only so for that moment.
Don't stare too far into the fire in order to attempt to find the warmth that is already embracing you.
Beauty is within you and with you.
Sit.
Accept and embrace.

—Craig Dawtrey

This is the beginning of a terrible nightmare. The only problem is that I am awake — unfortunately. I cannot switch my mind off.

At all.
At night.
At all.
During the day.
At all.
Never, ever off.

Eleven hours of sleep over eight consecutive days is the start of the decline and a cycle of insomnia.

> "Insomnia, also known as sleeplessness is a sleep disorder in which people have trouble sleeping. It is typically followed by daytime sleepiness, low energy, irritability, and a depressed mood. It can occur independently or as another problem such as psychological stress."
>
> —*Wikipedia*

Every sound bothers me. The swirling fan above the bed; the summer cricket's chirp, the wind, the traffic—everything adds to the sleepless torture. I've never been a great sleeper at the best of times, but this is ridiculous. My whole familial future whirls through my mind continuously.

Day-in and day-out.

What is my future with or without Jackie? We are in the enviable position at this stage of being able to kick back and take life easier, affording regular travel out of school semester. Both children have completed school, and this would give us time to explore the world and each other in depth. Is this still possible?

Does she still want to? I certainly still want to.

Shoved off a cliff, I am in free-fall. When I land, what will cushion the pain and the shock? Falling and watching as the last thirty years' memories scroll past on the cliff face in front of me as I descend.

When will I land? Will I land at all? At night, I turn across to see the dark profile of the one I love, not knowing if there was a tomorrow together. Tomorrow, when we awake. Or the day after.

I steal a glance at the profile that for so many years had brought comfort, support, and solace to me.

The image of the two of us on rocking chairs on the patio that Jackie had repeatedly said was the vision that had kept her convinced we would be together for life.

Gone?

This isn't the way it is meant to be. This is not what we had discussed!

"Maybe the script has changed," she flippantly croaks.

Just like that? I think.

I am stepping on butter, with every step insecure and unstable. As I slip, I hold my hand out for the reassuring touch from her that I had been so used to, only to have it ignored. There was a hole in my safety-net. I often noted how beautiful I still found her and not knowing what was still to come, I wrote:

> Daylight leaves us with shadowed faces
> As sleep slowly embraces
> The lines of life's experience

Etched ever so lightly
Upon your face
I trace your brow
Where frowns of concern and query have nested
My fingers touch your nose through which so many
Moments have passed
And left light and a delicate shadow
Tweaked with past disapprovals
Aside your eyes a crown of happiness
And laughter
And joy temporarily reside
These make me glad
As I know these are the good day's kiss
As our thoughts fade into sleep
We awake, and the lines are for now gone
This is slumber's idle gift

—Craig Dawtrey

THE FAMILY HOLIDAY

The extended family on my wife's side had celebrated December holidays every five years or so as Barry (one of her brothers), and his family had emigrated to Australia many years prior. The reunion-style holiday was always highly anticipated as the whole family of sixteen members would celebrate in a different city or even another country. The last one had been in France. This year, it was to be held in the small Cape village of Knysna.

We had spent many holidays in Knysna as Jackie's

parents had owned a home on Leisure Isle for decades and this was not only seen as a family reunion, but a re-visit to a well-known and much-loved place.

All the flights and accommodation had been booked prior to this marital fallout and affair, and so we had essentially committed to the holiday. At this stage, none of Jackie's family was aware of what had been going on with our shaky marriage. The four of us had all made an effort to keep it quiet for various reasons; much of which might have been similar to my concern—the hope that this could be saved before anyone outside of our home found out.

A few days before leaving for the holiday, Lisa and I discussed the merits of going at all, as we are both very involved in the emotional chaos this has created. We are drained and afraid of what might transpire when we're there. It would be a charade of happiness for us. Are we supposed to pretend that all is fine?

I stand in front of her desk and say to Jackie, "I don't think we are going with on the holiday."

"You can't do this so late," she responds. "What about the rest of the family?"

"How am I supposed to do this all through the holiday?" Sadness tears at me.

"We will handle it like two mature adults," Jackie calmly replies.

"I certainly don't know how to pretend that nothing is wrong," I continue.

I have always shown my emotions and if I tried to hide them, it would have been obvious to all, eventually.

How the hell am I supposed to pretend that all is fine when the mother of my children and the daughter and sister of the people we are going on holiday with, is having an affair and I have no idea if we are finished as a couple?

She is still making up her mind about our future and going through 'a process' mentored and spurred on by the person she is cheating with, and I have to be a mature adult.

Hell, I would love to be that, tough!

We agree to go along and try and make the best of it, nonetheless. I think that possibly, by being compliant and not argumentative, I might be able to influence her decisions and make her change her mind and stay with me.

The insomnia continues in Knysna, as my mind just does not switch off. The early morning finds me awakened at 4 a.m. each day by a fisherman towing his boat out of the residential complex with the rusty clatter of the boat trailer ripping the morning sun from behind the ocean.

At Jackie's behest, I must allow her to contemplate and walk on her own; she would invite me along when and if she was in the mood and ready on a certain day I comply, fearful of being disruptive and possibly worsening the situation—not knowing if it CAN at all be worsened. When I am honoured enough to be invited to walk with her, I try to hold her hand as we always did in the past. However, I can feel the fading responsiveness and unwillingness in her flaccid hand. Her love for me is fading daily and it is destroying me.

On New Year's Eve, we plan a walk to 'Dripkelders', a well-known trail in the Knysna forest that ends in beautiful, cool, clear fresh-water pools where we can all swim before going back along the same path to the parked cars.

Prior to leaving our accommodation and while preparing for the walk, Lisa notices that she has left her walking shoes at our home in Johannesburg. She comes through to talk to us, slightly embarrassed, and admits her mistake.

"Oh, god, Lisa. You are so damned disorganised!" Jackie rolls her eyes in disdain.

Lisa's eyes darken in sadness, and I can feel her heart sag as she resignedly follows up with, "Then I won't go with, mom."

She is being unfairly tongue-lashed by someone she has been keeping a secret from her own family.

I take Jackie aside and say to her in a quiet way just out of ear-shot, "Jackie, Lisa is going through this as much as you and I are. Stop being so hard on her."

"I will take Lisa and Robert into town and find a cheap pair of walking shoes and socks and then join the rest of you at the start," is my compromise.

We drive into town and find a one-hundred-and-forty-rand solution to the 'big' problem.

"Jeez, dad, why is mom so snappy?" Robert asks. I have no answer to give, but know the issue.

The rest of the family group drives ahead to the parking spot for the departure of the walk.

Jackie travels in one of the other cars as Lisa, Robert and I conclude the shoe shopping expedition. Once completed, we hop back into our rental car and start the approximately twenty-minute drive to the departure point's parking area. The rest of the family are still blissfully unaware of the events brewing behind-the-scenes.

Admittedly, at this stage, I am also still not aware of the full details myself. "Guys, how about we set up a WhatsApp group called Winning Mom Back and then we can see how we can make her happy and do good things so she misses us?"

"Sounds like a great idea, dad" they both respond to my suggestion and Lisa goes about setting up the group. Although we are saddened and shocked by what is transpiring in front of our eyes, we all want to keep her in the family and are desperate to win her back, genuinely believing she will make the 'correct' decision and realise she is straying onto the wrong path.

"I have an idea," Robert announced. "How about we treat her with small surprises and collectively make her feel wanted?" This will hopefully make her once again a part of our little fractured family... We are after all a team!

"Great idea, Robert. We are all in."

We join the awaiting group and start the stroll through the Knysna forest. It is a very hot summer's day, yet the heavily wooded undergrowth shelters us with mottled shadows and alternately cool breezes. As it is a single track, we have to walk in single file and without appearing too obvious I try to keep in close touch with Jackie. Her lack of enthusiasm and interest in reciprocation and eye contact scrapes at my heart. I cannot understand the absolute vacuum of feeling displayed to me. She is making no effort to even pretend to care. It is THAT obvious to me. But what am I to do?

Arguing serves no immediate purpose. Leaving the group exposes one as a sulk and abandons the children to themselves, and over-trying exposes one to smacking of desperation. Do I attempt to try and balance the Great Pyramid inverted on my head? So, I try.

Surly, non-participatory looks and alternate glances at her cell phone tell a tale; one that I don't want to believe, and so, pretend to ignore it for the afternoon. I slide into the mountain pool, immersing myself gently and baptismally hoping for respite from the oppressive heat.

"Come and join us, Jackie," I call out.

"It's too cold," is the chilly response.

After the swim and a nourishing snack, we start the return journey back along the path. Her body language is infinitely loud. Her interest in us is turned and away; selfish and introspective. It is her solution and her happiness that is being pursued at all costs. The decision has been made and had even been expressed as such in different family forums.

As the evening creeps in on us, dinner is prepared. The party starts with New Year's Eve sundowners on the patio as Jackie takes a photograph of the blushing setting sun and sends it off to Mark. Is this its destination?

It is after midnight and the alcohol has taken its toll on all. I broach the subject of the fake name and the message with Jackie. Her mute response and blank stare rips all the emotion from deep inside of me and I break down. As the deer-in-the headlights drives her horns into me, I sob.

"We're going home now!" I shout out, partially aware that this is impossible, as I am far too drunk to do that safely.

The three of us sleep in another house, away from Jackie, and in the morning, the news of the affair is known by all. We feel like pariahs.

I don't want to stay for the balance of the planned holiday, but nonetheless, force it on myself.

This impasse lasts for a few more days, including my birthday on January third. It is an earth-shatteringly awful birthday with my over-compensatory affection towards her appearing embarrassingly desperate and obvious to everyone else. I look and feel pathetic and this does nothing to help my self-esteem now.

The holiday ends with me taking a pill called Stresam (a non- benzodiazepine anxiolytic or anti-anxiety medication), as telephonically prescribed by my general practitioner. I hope this will help me sleep. Alas, it doesn't. All it does is precipitate panic attacks and a badly medicated routine which is destined to ultimately destroy my year of 2016.

MEDICINE'S INTRUSION

Back at home in Johannesburg and once again after several days without sleep, I call my general practitioner requesting an appointment in delirious desperation. Upon arrival in his rooms, I settle down in the seat opposite him and say, "Doctor, I need something to help me sleep. I am on the edge." I mean this literally, as it feels as if I am on the edge of a precipice, looking over into a dark abyss. I'm overcome by absolute exhaustion, and I have no idea how to beat it.

Exhaustion saps one's strength of mind and body. It sucks all resistance and ability to fight for survival until eventually, logic starts to desert sensibility. Concentration and efficiency wane and never wax back to normality if sleep is constantly absent. I am sensitive to every sound and movement. My mind will just not switch off. Many of my social advisors—both friends and family—try to guide me in the direction of relaxation and impossibly elusive sleep.

In the first three months since finding out what has happened to my marriage and family, my weight drops by ten kilograms. I had always been a healthy, fit, and strong man weighing 93 kilograms standing 1.85 m tall. I have never smoked and of course, loved an occasional cold, social beer—this is what I refer to as my only vice. However, I am advised not to drink any alcohol as it is a depressant, and can create other problems. And my 'only vice' is reduced to a minimum, reluctantly.

I also consult with a psychologist during a brief stint at psychotherapy and she also asked whether I had considered going onto anti-depressants.

This would apparently assist with the sleep once I had reached a semblance of normality in daily life. The anti-depressants will be "… a crutch to help you through whilst you are healing" I am told by the doctor and psychologist. Is this even an option?

I had never considered THAT medical path and had always been reluctant to take any medication unless it was absolutely necessary and there were no alternatives. If I had been ill in the past and if there was a risk of secondary infections due to neglected colds or flu, I would submit to the use of antibiotics. I knew when they were necessary. At this stage, I am so exhausted though that I am considering any sensible solution… It feels as if my life is collapsing around me.

The happy family of four is disintegrating to a family of one! Lisa is old enough and ready to leave home. At least, that was the plan for this year. Robert is supposed to start first year at university in January, and without Jackie there, I am going to be reduced to loneliness. Dinner for one… fuck, what now?

After a brief discussion of where I am emotionally and physically, I tell him, "Richard I don't want to take anything I can get hooked on."

He knows Jackie, and when he hears of the separation, he is as surprised as all the other family, friends, and for that matter, the extended family. We always had a great relationship, my doctor and I, and would often spend half the consultation time chatting and joking before getting down to the main business of medical advice. I generally knew what was wrong from my health perspective and would often go to him purely so that he could confirm my own diagnosis and prescribe the antibiotics if I really needed them...

"Ja, Craig, but I still deserve my fee!" he would joke. I always agreed with him, even if only for the fifteen minutes of laughter therapy in the consulting room. I often wondered what the other patients in the waiting room thought about the laughter emanating from inside.

"You don't have an addictive personality," he reminds me, and I imagine I'm hearing a questioning tone in the statement.

"No, I don't," I agree.

I had always had enough discipline to work when necessary, play when necessary, and more importantly, I knew when it was time to stop with both. He explains how the sad state or depression is a result of lowered serotonin, and how the antidepressants (SSRI's) should assist with resetting the serotonin to the correct level and improve my mood.

> "SSRI's are 'thought to' produce their effect through an initiating step of inhibition of the serotonin transporter leading to an increase in the synaptic levels of serotonin."
>
> —*Dr MA Horowitz, PhD, Prince of Wales Hospital; Sydney; Australia. Article in The Lancet Psychiatry, March 2019*

I contemplated the suggestion for a few moments and then—resigned to the assumption that my doctor is probably correct—trusting that all will be fine, I say, "Ok, I will try them then."

There is neither an awareness nor warning of any potential side-effects of psychotropic medication and I am only concerned about any potential addiction or dependence. I figure I will simply go onto the anti-depressants for a while until my life normalises (whatever that is), and then go off them once again. My ignorance about this side of the problem and medication was glaringly obvious in hindsight.

The script is pushed across the doctor's desk, settling a short arms-length away from me. "There you go. Let me know how it shapes up."

I pick it up nonchalantly, tuck it into my shirt pocket, and say, "Cheers, Richard, chat soon. Thanks for the help."

The short queue at the pharmacy dispensary clears out in front of me on that late afternoon and I, somewhat elatedly and trustingly, receive the medication from the pharmacist, having no doubt that these few pills in a small box will be the start of my healing and a path back to clarity.

Serdep, (or *Sertraline* is an SSRI or Selective Serotonin Uptake Inhibitor), is the first attempt at his suggestion and I start a course the same day, hoping for a quick remedy.

The first rule of depression and the poison they give you for it is this: there is no quick solution. All the doctors and psychiatrists would tell me the same thing, "Give it some time to work."

This waiting time for the medication to take effect could be anything from two to six weeks. To top it all off, there is no guarantee of success! If it doesn't work, then we will try something else... Another six weeks to attempt to find a happier space when you can't see past another day... You are so fucking sad and this is exacerbated by the exhaustion. But we will try. We will always try, because what is the alternative? Stay in depression, or get worse?

After about five days of taking the Serdep, I feel 'kak'. I feel worse than I had felt prior to taking any medication. My energy levels drop off dramatically and I start to feel down... really down. My heart pounds in my chest and I feel dull. I have a 'cottony' feeling in the mind—what us as South Africans would call 'dof'.

Fortunately, I have always been aware of my body and how it reacts to situations and influences from a medical perspective. As an enthusiastic sportsman, I had always been in control of how my body reacts to training and medication, as well as food and nutrition.

I know THIS is the medicine making me feel even more like shit... I am depressed and in a zombie zone. Recognizing this, I call my doctor.

"Richard, I feel really crap." After only five days, he takes me off the Serdep cold turkey, replacing it with Brintellix.

Thankfully, after about ten days, I start to feel a bit closer to normal. I can see some positivity in my life. But compared to what I had felt like for a few months, a kick in the crotch would have made me feel normal again. This medication, hopefully, was working.

> "Brintellix or Vortioxetine is a serotonin modulator. How it works is not entirely clear and is 'believed' to be related to increasing serotonin levels."
> – *Wikipedia*

EKUTHULENI

Early in January, after our return from the disastrous family holiday in Knysna, Jackie decides to stay at home for the month. Lisa is starting her first job as a teacher, and Robert is due to begin his first year of university. Jackie had initially wanted to take the first few weeks of January to move out for 'a few weeks' to contemplate her future with me.

I feel the timing is not good, and in truth, know there will NEVER be a 'good time' for her to do this… I want her to stay. It will have had a traumatic effect on the children, even though they are young adults now. They hurt as much no matter what their ages when they see a parent leave their home. It is supposed to be the other way around, after all, with children leaving the nest! Our situation has now deteriorated dramatically.

Jackie has degraded our hugs and mutual "I love you" to "I love you, Jackie" from me and a "You too" from her.

It further reduces to "I love you, Jackie" and I wince at the slap-in-the-face response from her, "Thank you".

"Thank you!"

Fuck you! is what I want to say, yet I hold it back, always hoping to save the what-by-now appears unsalvageable.

Jackie tells me, "I have booked to go to a Buddhist retreat at Ekuthuleni for two days of contemplation." This is not unusual, as she has done this on numerous occasions in the past.

I say to her, "Shouldn't I go with you?" At least we can discuss our marriage situation together, and with luck, find a positive solution?" I am prepared to try anything… meditate, chant, grow a pony-tail, wear a kaftan, or even shove a lit cracker up my—by now, edgy—back-side.

The answer from Miss Out-Of-Control is, "No, Craig, I need to do this on my own."

So, I give her the space she apparently needs. I watch her as she packs her weekend bag, and I walk her to the car that Friday afternoon.

With a kiss on the cheek, she takes another piece of my soul as she reverses out of the driveway. The lack of care that trails in her wake says so much, but I am trying not to listen.

It hurts too much.

Our weekend passes uneventfully, and two days later she returns dragging her weekend bag into the house looking no worse-for-wear compared to when she had left. She does, however seem very hasty in going to the bedroom. There are no hugs or kisses for me, Lisa, or Robert. There are no "how are you's" and no inquiries about our weekend.

She drifts in, walks up the stairs and goes to her study. This does NOT feel good. The only emotion she brought along—cold indifference—is being dragged behind her up the stairs. The evening carries on uneventfully and after supper and watching some television as a family, we go to bed.

No hugs, no kisses, no "I love yous". Just somnolence for one, and insomnia for the other.

The early morning light peeks through the thick curtain as we prepare for the new morning. I am hopeful for new opportunities and marital salvation. Once our children have left for school and university and the atmosphere is clear, I pose the fatal question.

I ask her, "How was the break? Have you made a decision?" I am still ever-hopeful that the considered answer will be, "I am staying and want to make a go of this marriage again."

Her answer is, "I still need a few weeks on my own to see how I feel."

My heart sinks. This does not sound good to me at ALL! I always knew that if I had 'allowed' her to leave—if only for a few days, or weeks—that it would be the end. Yet, how does one disallow another from making her own choices without being controlling? I have no choice but to agree.

"If you love it set it free
If it comes back to you it's yours
If it doesn't it never was."

Or alternatively, "Hunt it down and kill it."

The latter, sadly, is not an option.
As humans, we need to make the choice of:
Spending a lifetime in jail;
A lifetime in chains;
Or a lifetime!?

We arrange how to tell the children that their mother is still going to stay in a separate place to make some decisions. My soul collapses. It crawls deep inside my chest and cowers.

That evening, we sit at the dinner table. We dine uncomfortably for the last time as a family; yet, we don't know it at this point. It is stilted, controlled, and sad.

We had always committed to supper times at the dinner table, and over the twenty years with children, stuck happily to this discipline. Sitting and eating in front of the television was never an option, as this would interfere in communication and family-friendly banter. One… last… time.

The last remnants of food are scraped off the plates as we drag the inevitable conclusion from under the table and the sad topic is broached.

"Mom is going to stay at Nicholas's cottage for a few weeks to sort out a few things," I announce.

"I will be in contact every day with you," is her reassurance to them. Yet, the reassurance holds no weight.

We tell the children the bad news. My daughter looks at my drawn face and says, "Don't worry, dad, we will be fine."

She is pacifying and protecting me. She has seen, felt, and joined the injured soul. Both the children are feeling the agonising pain and are unable to interpret it as well, so they bumble along with me. They miraculously manage to hold back the tears, but I can see the pain in their eyes as they look at me and collectively wonder what this means for now AND the future of us all.

Jackie suggests that, as it is not a great night, she should probably move out immediately. She walks up the stairs, packs a bag, and moves into the cottage on our premises.

No more than five metres separates the main house from the cottage, and with the curtains slightly open, I despairingly look across the stark brick-work where I can see her talking to someone on the phone. No doubt to the one who is 'helping her through the process'. She seems quite animated if not elated as she communicates the 'small victory' of her decision to the ear on the other end of the telephone. It is with heavy hearts that Robert, Lisa, and I go to bed that evening.

The next day, she moves out from our house and into her brother's cottage as he and I had felt that there, she would be safe and secure. My children and I feel it is also better not to communicate with her at this time; if she wants to move out, she should feel what the emotional isolation could be like away from family. At least for a few days.

This communications embargo is difficult to

maintain, as I continue receiving news about her movements from mutual friends who sadly say that she is taking Mark as company to events and functions. I am sure 'just as friends' ...

Lisa mentions to me shortly after Jackie's move that she might want to let Mark's wife know what is going on. She says that if that had been happening to her, she would want someone to tell her, to avoid the embarrassment it causes for the victim of infidelity. I am not convinced she should do this, but nonetheless, make no effort to stop her as she is an adult woman of twenty-three years and has her own mind.

Lisa and her boyfriend decide to set up a false Facebook profile to contact Susan, Mark's wife. The message reads somewhat like this..."Hi, you don't know me, but your husband is having an affair with my mother."

A few days pass by when Lisa confides in me that the profile had been set up, a message had been sent, and she had received a response from Susan.

Needless to say, Susan is distraught. Mark's wife sadly and reluctantly confirms this possibility; yet, she is still unconvinced that he is cheating on her again—this had happened twice before with two other women according to her—and in my opinion, she is in denial.

Lisa calls me aside one evening and says, "Dad, Susan said you can call her if you need to talk about this situation."

Shit, I don't want to; but for me, the reality of what might be happening is so much worse than pretending nothing untoward is going on!

"Thanks, Lisa. I guess I should?"

So, I agree and call her.

A shaky, gentle voice answers. The strange number prods her heart as it flashes across the screen of the phone. It is a phone call that neither of us really want to make. "Hi, is that Susan?"

"Yes…Craig?"

"This is Craig. I am sorry, but I am not sure what to say here."

Yet, we continue talking slowly and carefully. After confirming a few details about what we are aware of, she confirms that Mark has been going to similar functions as Jackie, but only as 'a client'. We are both being hoodwinked, lied to, cheated on, and betrayed. We are two souls briefly linked together in heartache and confusion.

Since the beginning of this desperate process, support from my brother-in-law has been incredible. I am still working for him, and he needs an efficient employee and a functioning, contented family member. He does not take sides, but has been witness to the whole escapade.

He counsels me and says, "You need to stay in contact with Jackie and show strength in order to woo her back."

He is convinced that this will work. She is his sister, after all, and as such I value his advice. That evening, I return home to my fractured family from the factory, and happily say to Lisa, "I am going to chat to mom, and this is how I am going to win her back."

I see Lisa's eyes break contact with mine, and I ask

her, "What, Lisa?"

Looking back up again, she says to me sadly, "Dad, I don't know how to tell you this, but mom went to Ekuthuleni with Mark!"

My legs drain of energy once AGAIN.

"How do you know?" I say sadly.

"I spoke to Susan and she told me mom picked him up and they went on a business trip."

I call Jackie immediately and ask her, "Did Mark go with you to Ekuthuleni?"

Her defensive retort is, "No, absolutely not! Craig, I want to know where is this coming from."

Denial. I pose the question once again, this time pressing aggressively, as I don't believe her. She denies it yet again, and I persist until, in a fit of anger, she snaps, "Yes, I picked him up and gave him a lift as he had a function in the same area!"

Yes, sure. Pressure had exposed the lie AGAIN.

According to her story, he had NOT gone to Ekuthuleni with her. They coincidentally had "different functions in the same area".

I want to believe this, but my faith and trust in her is gone.

A day later, I decide to clear this issue up and needing to know the truth, I call Ekuthuleni to find out if he had accompanied her to the retreat.

"Good morning," I say to the lady who answers the phone.

"Good morning," is the polite response from the other end.

I continue, "I have two clients that love your retreat

and I am considering spoiling them with a weekend away and need to know if they had been there this year. I would like it to be special, and if they had been this year, then I would consider it too much of a duplication and not a surprise." This is, of course, a lie fabricated to get around the client confidentiality issue with the retreat.

"Please could you let me know if they have been there this year?" I continue.

She politely consults the visitor's book and replies, "No, neither of them has been here this year!"

On the one hand, this response could have been positive; but sadly, the implication is that Jackie and Mark's collective lie was even bigger, and that neither of them had been to Ekuthuleni.

My anger sweeps my children under its wings as they have also been under the impression that their mother had gone for a contemplative retreat for her AND for the family. It is a betrayal of our children's trust as well.

Is this the same person I had been with for so long, and had loved and believed for decades? Who is this individual? What had become of that lady I once knew?

Jackie had taken to meditation several years before, and I always noted how, at the end of the meditation session she would, with her hands in prayer, touch her forehead, then her mouth, and lastly her heart. I asked her what this meant, and she told me it indicated "congruency, the state where what a person thinks, says, and does is at one, and is thus congruent."

In a fit of anger and realisation I shout at her, "YOU ARE NOT CONGRUENT! WHAT YOU SAY AND DO ARE NOT IN SYNCH! YOU ARE A LIAR AND A HYPOCRITE!"

I had learnt from the teacher and coach, and used her self-implicating words in return.

The adage 'practice what you preach' comes to mind. At this stage, I am still hoping Jackie has just made one silly mistake and will come to her senses and back to the family. I am, of course, very wrong.

This was never to happen. The deception was continuing unabated, although she would deny she was seeing him.

———

In good faith, I continue with this medical regime and my 'normal' life of work, cooking supper, trying to sleep, and maintaining some form of positivity in the depleted household.

It is increasingly difficult to manage a home where, for twenty-five years, I had had the domestic burden split between two, namely my wife and myself. Now, I must plan and execute everything on my own. Not progressively, but instantaneously.

With time during the day limited, I am finding it difficult to continue my normal exercise regime. Exercise and the concomitant production of endorphins is highly advised for depression and sleep disorders, and I am starting to lose the benefits of that influence. Along with the reducing exercise, my motivation drops off. Lack of exercise and sadness is becoming a vicious circle with one problem feeding the other.

On the odd late afternoon, I bravely attempt a run for a few kilometres around my neighbourhood, returning sweaty and relatively elated.

"How did that go, dad?" my children chime.

"Pretty good, actually... I will do this every second day, I think," is my positive response.

In my late twenties, I had completed two Iron Man Ultra triathlons and was extremely fit, however, the toils and hardship of a race that long had put me off any endurance sport for a long time.

I know cardiovascular exercise is the better option for depression, but I actually hate running. It is too boring and builds no muscle. I am afraid that if I continue running, I will lose even more weight, and I need to increase my muscle mass. So, there are several reasons swaying me away from the road.

Sleep continues to evade me, and the weight keeps dropping off. Never in my life did I think I would have a problem maintaining my weight. A lifetime of healthy eating and a fair participation of the 'Bavarian Barley juice' saw to that.

I try hot baths with various bath salts, even though I dislike bathing—I much prefer a quick shower. I add Epsom salts and whatever else is suggested, be they aromatic or sterile. I don't care for opinions, but only for suggestions… I am so inexperienced in self-indulgent bathing aromatherapy.

I bath until I sweat, and while I wallow miserably in the bath-made-for-two-but-occupied-by-one I hum like a Buddhist, chant like a chemically-infused Shaman, and mumble affirmations and incantations to the ceiling above the bath. The plaintive whale-like-sounds echo around the small bathroom as they search for some solace or an answer to the pleading questions being asked.

Simple things like, "What the fuck?"

The candles flicker, shamelessly casting mobile shadows against the walls, and bounce off the mirrors as their flames lick and raise their bobbing heads over the edge of the bath as they peer at my middle-aged nakedness, hoping to see who is making the strange sounds that allow them to sway and dance. The apparition in the bath ignores them for a while as the candles weigh up their options and peer at each other unreassuringly, hoping that one will make a call and save what is left of their waxen lives.

They dance and glance until the person that lies there tires of their presence, and then waits until the water cools down to a tepid, unsoothing conclusion. Shusshhhhhh… It is then time to get out.

The cooled water slides off my skin, sinking into the bath mat on the tiled floor as I dry myself with a thick, soft towel and slowly pull on a set of warm pyjamas and a gown. I try to pamper myself back into shape through unfamiliarly self-indulgent means and behaviours as I soak the water from the floor and from my drained spirit until I move on to the next stage of sleep-preparation.

The next process on my nocturnal list is attempting to apply relaxation techniques which I have been taught by one of the psychologists I had consulted. These techniques work only moderately well. To be honest, they don't work well at all, but here goes...

I sit on the chair alone in my bedroom with the lights off and then alternately tense and relax my muscles, starting from the toes and progressing upward; I repeat the action with each muscle group in the front of my body and then the back.

Tense... then relax... whilst saying as I breathe out, "everything is going to be fine". Breathe in for the next stage ... and...Then, with the feet pointed downward toward the ground, tense... and relax... long breath out, "Everything is going to be fine". Calf muscles... thighs... abdominals... chest... neck... and then...

Finally, my face contorts with the strangest expressions as I wince, smile, and grimace my way through the facial muscles... I must look ridiculous, but the lights are off, my children are downstairs AND "everything is going to be fine"... It isn't fine... not for a LONG time. But I try.

After the bathing and relaxation techniques are complete, I delay until late in the evening the process of going to sleep, trying to make bedtime the same every day. I was advised to adopt a routine and never sway from that routine. Nothing seems to work and life starts to become mundane, dull, and predictable.

My doctor suggests that I take a Dormonoct (Loprazolam) to go to sleep, and a half a Dormicum (Midazolam) under my tongue for fast effect if I wake up early and struggle to go to sleep again. This IS the case and as he is my trusted general practitioner,

I go for it! I sleep well for a few hours, but awake with a start every morning at about 2 am. The half a Dormicum under the tongue helps for a further two hours or so, but I never feel rested the next day. The drowsiness continues as the half-life of the medication saps my energy.

Talk about cut-and-paste! A great big turd-plaster in the face of sleep. What's the point? But I try this for a while to no avail. It was only many months later that I found out these are both benzodiazepines and are used for;

> "...anaesthesia procedural sedation, sleeping trouble and severe agitation."
> —*Wikipedia*

During the drug-induced slumber, one's mind is not actually in deep sleep and is defined by the British Journal of Anaesthesia as, "...causing a loss of ability to create new memories, or Anterograde Amnesia". So, you are out cold, but not asleep and resting!

The body becomes used to the dose due to tolerance withdrawal and unless the dose is increased by the doctor, sleep worsens again. The choice is mine. Hating the thought of taking this poison, but feeling the need for sleep and recovery, I constantly toil with the "should I or shouldn't I" quandary.

I am trying to work a full day's job within the family business (her family's) and pretending to be a capable father to my two adult children who are devastated by their mother leaving the home and their sad dad who is struggling to be supportive of them when he feels he can't put one foot in front of the other.

It is during these first few months in hell that I discover my absolute hatred of the call of the African Hadeda (Grey Ibis). These native South African birds have the unenviable ability to make a god-awful noise as the sun rises and repeating the effort at sunset, reminding you daily that you have another day to fight through or another night battling sleeplessness —ugly, noisy bastards.

To this day, I think it is the only bird I actually hate (along with the sound of a cricket somewhere in the damn room!) Haaa! Haaa! Haaa! SHUT THE FUCK UP, please.

It seems at the time of sadness, that nature in all its variety suddenly disguises its beauty and conspires against you personally to torture you with sleep deprivation. I happen to get them out of the bloody Jacaranda tree in my garden for quite a while by utilising mother nature's other gift... the lemon.

There was a beautiful lemon tree in the garden that would produce about five hundred lemons twice a year; that is a thousand very useable lemons from one tree. They went down well with hot water, tequila, and pelting the shit out of Hadedas in my garden.

They were better than stones, because if they landed on the neighbour's car, they wouldn't damage it. And, of course, it could be seen as a generous donation from the neighbour who was losing touch with his normality!

I start limiting my movements to my now partially-deserted house, as my wife has by now slowly moved her clothes out of our walk-in closet. I can see our marriage draining away dress by dress, spaces in the closet stretching wider and darker along with the approaching winter.

The house grows colder as the life is slowly sucked out of it along with winter's frigid intrusion. The sun is rising later, but the alarm goes off at the same time every day as routine forces me to keep going. Physically, darkness partners up with emotional shadow as they hug and collude, bringing sadness deeper into my life. Nature has no sympathy, and she goes about her business with the timing and pace that she needs.

A few days later, I receive a message on my cellular phone, "I need to collect some of my winter clothes. It's getting cold". The text includes cute, patronising little emojis of snow and snowmen. I look at the Emojis with hope and seek some positive hidden meaning to pick me up.

"Of course, you can collect them," I respond; they are only a few clothes after all. I accept the request, never doubting that the clothes would return with her to our home soon.

The clothes never did return. They stayed away forever, just like the person they intermittently draped. Bright interspersed colours are exchanged for ever-increasing dark spaces. Dresses, blouses, and shirts hang forlorn with their coat-hanger thinned shoulders, sadly inanimate; rejected shoes cower shoulder- to-shoulder on the floor, their tongue-less mouths agape, unable to voice their confusion. Is it their scuffed heels and aging, wrinkled cheeks that have caused this? Why are THEY the ones to be left behind?

One afternoon, I notice the closet seems a bit more tightly packed, but with different clothes that I somehow recognise.

"Lisa, why are your clothes in my cupboard?"

My daughter responds brightly, "To lessen the empty space, dad."

Only to protect her father. My heart soars and aches as I hug her and whisper, "Thanks, Lisa."

This was not her battle, yet she was conscripted through birth and then the separation of her parents to stand on the frontline of the cold war that was starting to entrench itself in our home. She hates to see the sadness in her father's eyes, and I hate to see it in hers. Symbiotic sadness moves into the home as we try to replace the woman who has left us.

The king-size bed feels so wide as I squeeze into one corner, careful not to disturb the ghost sleeping next to me. And think amidst tears…

> So,
> The once strong shell
> Bolstered by family coatings of reinforcement and strength
> Slowly broken down, layer by layer with age
> And its extractions from normality
> Reset
> But how?
> The shell is thinner
> The resistance is lower

The will to survive is higher but to thrive is being dragged down
Like a fishing net
Searching for sustenance but constantly being snagged on reefs
So full of opportunity
But hooking and holding onto life's anchors
The drive forward
Held and tempted
But
Oh
Where
To
From
Here?

—*Craig Dawtrey*

ANOTHER DAY

Summertime and the living is easy... not. Another day of trying to be normal and being brave for the kids, as my by-then absent wife had said I should be. Hmm, so what does that entail? Get up after absolutely no sleep, thinking, *I wonder if I can save or resuscitate the love and marriage.*

Make up half a bed, as the ghost once again has not disturbed her side. Go to work and try to pretend there is nothing wrong and still something worth saving. Be careful not to let the people at work notice you are not the same happy person you used to be. But I can't be false. So, I avoid interaction with my co-workers as much as possible.

Planning mealtimes becomes an issue, as I have never had to do that. This shouldn't be too difficult, so here I go. I make use of our domestic worker's culinary abilities wherever I can. She has been with us for over twenty years, and I have inherited her along with the children, cats, and house. I ask her to cook basic suppers and whatever I cannot prepare for the depleted family myself.

Lisa tries to help me for a while by acting as a surrogate mother to Robert, and emotional and catering partner to me. It is not her responsibility or role, but she does it instinctively. Wrongly, I accept.

I must plug the emotional hole with anything I can find, and I snap up my daughter's assistance with getting a semblance of normality into the home. It is an unintended cruelty imposed on her, as she is struggling with her own demons at the time, and is also trying to make some sense of what has happened. Her mother had also walked out of her home, and she had seen all the tears that had ensued, both during and after the immediate chaos.

I ask her for advice on how to handle the relationship with Jackie, which is also dividing her allegiance. It is asking too much of someone that young and as entrenched in the situation. I know this, but also hope that by using her as a sounding board, I can reach some logical conclusion and temporary solutions to get out of the place in which I am trapped. Perhaps she could see something that I might have missed that could remedy or at least reduce the hurt. I need to read to distract myself from the problem at hand and not to ruminate, yet I crave the company of my family around me.

Covering both needs, I take my book into Lisa's room and read on her bed or couch whilst she watches TV. Even though she doesn't complain, I am unintentionally bringing my sadness into her space and infecting her.

I try to exchange beds with Robert, and he tries a

few nights in my bed upstairs whilst I try his on the ground floor. The situational change however cannot break the sadness or help with sleep. After only two nights, we go back to our own beds.

The psychiatrist advised me not to watch any television after 8p.m. so-as to avoid any over-stimulation of my mind, which would likely disrupt my sleep. As a result of this, I bring my book into the TV room and sit with my back to the television to be with my children. It certainly doesn't help at all. There are too many restrictions imposed on me. I am forgetting how to relax and just live.

Someone else also hints that I should try and listen to Delta or Beta wave music to help me relax and fall asleep. I crawl into bed, desperately hopeful after reading for an hour, and gently place my headphones over my ears, plugging the jack into my iPad. Searching for a suitable tune takes a few minutes.

Selecting the longest one, it plays for as long as an hour as I lie with my eyes closed and the bedroom lights off. It creates a semblance of relaxation, and if I fall asleep, I will inevitably wake up again with a start when the music finishes. The music is relaxing, but embedded in the relaxation, is sadness. This merely exacerbates the woeful feeling of isolation I am sinking into as I lie in a dark room with the lights off while quiet, relaxing, sad music plays in my head. Cutting through the noise with a blunter blade merely dulls the pain a little bit more.

An hour later, I am awake again, but it is now an hour closer to arising for work. I now must try the conventional way of going to sleep, namely closing my eyes, and hoping for the best. Alternatively, trying half a sleeping pill, it is now realistically getting too late to take one and the net result is that I am still drowsy in the morning and even more dysfunctional at work.

I spend the first few hours of every day trying to wake my body up. If this doesn't work then I get up, go downstairs, and make a cup of tea. Peeking into my children's rooms as I pass, I am selfishly hopeful that one of them will be awake and willing to keep me company.

They are inevitably fast asleep as I sadly scan their shadowed features. Curled up in quiet, peaceful sleep, it betrays the reality of the trauma they are feeling.

Their home had been deserted by their mother and progressively emotionally deserted by their father as he retreated into sad self-pity. I hate this guilty feeling but still have no idea how to rid myself of it in the support for my children.

I shuffle up the stairs to the empty bedroom and try to sleep once again. The ceiling fan stirs the warm South African summer air over my bed and taunts me, keeping me from sleep with its whispering blades. The summer crickets maliciously team up with the fan by continuously 'chirping' from their concealed spaces.

Dazedly, I wander down to the kitchen in an attempt to find the insect spray, proceeding to 'carpet bomb' the whole room, hoping to silence the little bastards! They inevitably win the battle and I retire, defeated beneath the duvet once again. Lights off, and let's try once more.

After a few months on the Brintellix and having not felt any benefits, I call the general practitioner and say to him, "Doctor, I don't feel that the medication is helping. My sleep has not improved, and I am still feeling down, so I don't think it is working."

He responds with, "If you don't want to be on it anymore, then halve the pill for a week and then if you feel okay, throw the rest away."

The possibility of being off the anti-depressants appeals to me immensely, so I adopt his recommendation and after a week, stop the Brintellix altogether! If I had known what I know today about going off psychotropic medication, I would have stopped myself right there and then. This was as close as dammit to going off *'cold-turkey'*.

> "'Cold turkey' refers to the abrupt cessation of a substance dependence and the resulting unpleasant experience as opposed to the gradual easing of the process, and can be extremely dangerous."
>
> —Wikipedia

Not a week later, the panic attacks start viciously. There is no warning and no trigger for them to happen. They just descend—terrifyingly strongly and debilitatingly—and are described as *"sudden periods of intense fear that may include palpitations, sweating, shaking, shortness of breath, numbness or a feeling that something bad is going to happen."*

Breathless and fearful, I call a psychiatrist, hoping she might have a solution as she is more qualified than my general practitioner. After a twenty-minute discussion, she prescribes Remeron (a mirtazapine) for me. According to her, this will help with the depression, panic attacks, and with the sleep.

> "Mirtazapine is a tetracyclic anti-depressant... has strong antihistamine effects... how it works is not clear, but it may involve blocking certain adrenergic and serotonin receptors."
> —*Wikipedia*

Instead, it gives me terrifying nightmares. The confusion between what is causing this starts creeping into my thoughts. Is it the new medication, or the effects of withdrawal from the previous regime? Still hopeful and trusting the psychiatrist's advice, I continue with the mirtazapine.

One Sunday morning, I find myself in the kitchen putting pen to paper as a shopping list grows when suddenly I panic. I am shaking and crying; not sobbing, but more like a person afraid of battle.

Shit, I just had a panic attack because I had to do the grocery shopping for the first time as a potential single person! Confrontation with the unknown—or even a known contest where the foe is all-powerful—and the participants are going to be severely tested. We approach the task expecting little chance of victory.

Grocery shopping had never been an issue, and in my opinion, an exercise equitably shared with Jackie from a let's-go-and-do-it perspective. Yet, I found myself terrified of going on my own to do this menial task. After a discussion and reassurance from Lisa, I slip into my car anyway, as the panic slowly subsides.

Starting from the right, I work through the aisles of the grocery shop with the pencilled list for the week ahead facing upward in the shopping cart, all the time trying to make a mental menu for the next few days' meals.

It feels lonely and I am momentarily enviously distracted by the other apparently happy couples who had made it there together. I walk past the refrigerated section where the fish and meat are, and the cold air sends a shiver of emptiness down my spine. It all looks and feels so different compared to the few weeks before when we were there as a team.

A few days later, I receive an all-too infrequent telephone call from Jackie. Seeing the name of the caller appearing on the screen now causes a feeling of anxiety and sadness.

"Hi, Craig. We need to get together to clarify some separation issues and the home."

I hate that word. 'SEPARATED', as it signifies failure to me. It signifies sadness. I can't and don't want to say the word. It had never formed a part of my vocabulary, and I sure as hell wasn't going to include it at this stage. Although I would have loved to avoid the discussion, I have to accede.

Unsurprisingly, the conversation is awkwardly clipped and to the point. I needed clarity about what was happening with the family as it stood...

There was no doubt that our children wanted to stay with me and in any event, Jackie was showing no intention of finding them a place to stay with her. On the contrary, she was insinuating that they move to their own place or in with friends if I couldn't care for them—and as it turned out later, I was incapable of looking after them myself.

"And the cats?" I ask.

"Well, sort them out yourself," comes the selfish retort. "I don't want the cats and I have no space for them." The children could also not stay with Jackie, as her flat was not big enough! It sounds so simple when normality shrouds life, but when the disruption of torment steps in, everything seems daunting.

"But, Jackie, WHAT ABOUT THE HOUSE?"

"Put it up for sale!" another cold and callous reply cuts me down.

"Everything is going to change, Jackie!"

"Craig, nothing will change. You are still the father of my parent's grandchildren."

But alas, everything changes, and it changes forever. Family dynamics are upturned, uprooted, and destroyed. Interpersonal relationships are clipped and choked. Mutual friends take sides in divided support, armed only with their limited and one-sided information.

An emotional hurricane sweeps in and batters a family island chain, making the islands less inhabitable, and the crossing between them precariously hazardous. The islands can regenerate, but will never look or be the same. The trees will remain bent and scarred; some will die, and new ones will form. The buildings will be patched, and roofs will shelter the new inhabitants from recycled showers. Yet, the floors will always have remnants of a broken foundation. Stability, fractured.

It was about at this time that a huge Highveld thunderstorm crept in. It is an incredibly passionate contest between the devil and the clouds with the earth acting as its vocal victim. It is violent and beautiful, quiet, and raucous. Thunder and lightning combine to tear torrents of rain down to the ground to bond with sand and grass, trees, and life... and occasionally bringing death. The dry ground rapidly dampens and soaks and once saturated, the surface flows with torrents of water. Now complete, the liquid hastily seeps into the ground and leaves deep puddles, lifting the aroma of damp, nourishing soil. It is a joyous assault on the senses. This day, it was not good.

Oh, shit! The lightning destroyed the electric fence and the satellite television dish at the same time! That, was not the major issue. It was just that it was ANOTHER one. The final straw that buckled the camel's back... not broken yet!

I cry out of frustration at the perceived unfairness of it all, and the next morning, call the maintenance man to fix the problem. I can well do without any additional financial issues adding to the emotional ones!

A pity he couldn't fix a fractured family, I think.

Another day and another night passes. And again. At about 4 am one autumn morning, I hear an odd sound. Is that water flowing? A little too consistent.

A little too fast.

No-one in my house baths at this time of the day, is my first thought. Please, no?!

Cradling a flashlight, I traipse downstairs, open the back door, step outside, and glance up at the roof. Lo-and-behold, water is pouring out the overflow valve from the hot water heater as if Noah had planned a reunion. There is so much water that I can see the Ark docked on the gutter with the animals lining up two-by-two, awaiting their turn for boarding.

Fuck, not again?!

By switching off the hot water heater, I manage to stop the uncontrolled heating of the element which had boiled the water. It appears as if the thermostat has failed. This forces hundreds of litres of hot water onto the roof and into the garden, creating another expense and another kick in the down-there! Sighing with despair, I go back inside to get ready for work, fully aware that there is no more time for sleep.

The shutting down of my mind and body reflects in my daily living pattern, with my space and realm closing in tighter and tighter around me. It is a whirlpool spiralling inward, dragging me downward as it drowns me in sad isolation. Much of this isolation had started at my place of work.

I had been in the sales environment for over twenty years, and had never been afraid of people or crowds. In fact, I thrive amongst people; yet, this human interaction was becoming an issue. One of my duties was to travel domestically in South Africa and internationally to Namibia to consult with architects and electrical engineers on large lighting projects. It started with an anxiety towards visiting clients. I found myself not wanting to fly or drive to consult at all.

Socially, I stop going out at night and on the weekends, whether I had to drive or not.

The travelling and interaction are too stressful to handle, and the anxiety compounds these feelings.

"Join me at the Highland gathering, Craig," Alan coaxes. He plays the bag-pipes in a Scottish pipe-band and I have always wanted to attend a Highland Gathering. Joining them, I spend the afternoon with another friend of mine as well as my son at the Gathering and after its conclusion, enjoy a few beers to end the afternoon off.

Once the Gathering concludes with the final mass-parade out the way, I invite him to join me at home for a bite to eat. I need the company, as both my son and daughter are out with friends for the night, and Alan is a calming, fun influence. Shortly after arriving home and having eaten, I feel the anxiety return. This time, aggressively.

The evening drags on as the anxiety persists until eventually, it is time for my friend to go home, a thought that terrifies me. I ask random, irrelevant questions of him in an attempt to stall his departure. I just don't want to be alone.

At about 11:30 pm I eventually allow him to leave. Closing the front door, I slink up to bed hoping for some badly needed sleep, needing to escape from the pain and fear of the reality of my situation. Popping another ineffective sleeping pill, sleep once again doesn't arrive, along with the fear and anxiety refusing to retreat.

Every day, I find myself getting up later and later, and arriving at work after official starting time. Once at the factory and seated at my desk, I stare at the computer as my sad mind keeps drifting off into a contemplative freeze. After a few minutes, I snap back to the present, trying to work further; but frankly, I am becoming very unproductive.

I am fortunate that I have forged good relationships with my clients, and they don't need regular office visits from me, as business could be attended to via telephone and email. More detailed project discussions necessitated face-to-face meetings and I coerce myself to them, fighting through the stress.

I stay on target with my sales, but it is obvious to my peers that there is an issue with me.

I don't want everyone to know what the issue is or even that there is an issue, frankly; my wife is still a share-holder of the company and the sister of the managing director, my brother-in-law! What an almightily fucked-up and convoluted situation.

My deflated demeanour and rapid weight loss contribute to many theories about what is wrong in my life. How does one announce this to three hundred people who all know you and your wife? Imagine the questions and whispers in the corridors.

"They seemed so happy!"

"What did he do?"

"What did she do?"

This was nothing to be proud of and announce

to all, but all would come to know, eventually. This disastrous situation was to change my whole life and it was just a matter of time before the cracks started to show.

My father-in-law regularly visits the factory as he consults at the business, sharing his immense experience in the production process. It also gives him an interest and a purpose, as he is already over seventy-years old. The three of us have a brief meeting in my brother-in-law's office to tell him the bad news that Jackie has moved out. Being a proud family man, this is almost as hard on him as it is on me.

Over the next few weeks, the close contact between us becomes increasingly brief and stilted as the situation between my wife and I worsens with the end-result now seeming dismally obvious.

"Do you talk to each other much?" he wonders out aloud to me.

I respond with a, "No, hardly ever."

How am I to pretend to be happy and capable whilst crossing the path of my father-in-law and brother-in-law every day in the passage of work?

I wasn't the one who had crossed the marital boundaries, but as a close friend said to me, "Craig, blood is thicker than water."

Their support would inevitably drift over to her side as ultimately, she was their direct family. Why should I have been surprised?

The invitations to family gatherings for birthdays are the first ones to exclude me.

My mother-in-law's birthday was in February, and

this was the first time I felt the isolation.

I make a telephone call to my mother-in-law, and it goes unanswered, so I leave a message. A texted response from her confirms the message had been received. But that is all.

My children prepare to join the family festivities whilst, for the first time in thirty years, I am not invited.

"See you later, dad. Will you be okay?"

"Yes, Lisa, I will be fine," I lie. "Off you go now, and have fun. Send my love to everyone."

As they leave out of our driveway, I know they are once again torn between two families... victims still. Staring down the road after the car with my children in, I stand for a few moments.

One person rejected. This hurts. Painfully.

Separation from a whole family. Instantaneously. Her family. My family.

I think if you are the one to cause the break-up in a relationship it must be expected that rejection will follow from those that feel affected. There will understandably be animosity shown towards you. But when it is not your fault and the whole of that side of your family—including your children—are going to a family function, and you are not, it hurts like hell. Like a child gated for a crime he did not commit. Will you ever be freed and welcomed back into the fold?

In the past, the four of us would have happily piled into one car and journeyed through to the function. But it was now gone. Forever.

Everything changes! echoed in my head again. *Everything.*

It is early March, and Robert's birthday arrives. We agree to do dinner together. Just the four of us. This sounds promising.

"Would you like me to collect you and give you a lift?" I offer Jackie cautiously, not knowing what answer I want.

"No, thanks. Don't worry I will make my own way there," is the casual response.

Robert, Lisa, and I travel together to the restaurant in my car as Jackie uses Uber to make her own way there. This function is going to be difficult, but I will do this for my son.

Arriving at the restaurant a bit earlier than Jackie, we sit down at a table and wait, chatting nervously. At this stage, I am still hoping for some kind of reconciliation.

Eventually, she walks through the entrance as we politely stand up to give her a cursory kiss of welcome and sit down for dinner. The expressive gesticulation of busy hands brings my attention to her ring finger. I do a double-take of disbelief and then dejectedly pretend not to notice that the engagement and wedding bands are missing. My heart sinks as I retreat into myself.

Selfishly heart-sore, I find my personality retreat out of the restaurant and into the darkness outside. Too tired to chase it, I sink into silence, my eyes shifting slowly to my ring finger where the gold band she gave me twenty-seven years earlier still clings on hopefully.

We are still married and we have had no discussion about the removal of wedding rings; yet, a unilateral decision has been made with no consideration of the potential consequences and impact on others. A pattern was developing.

For me, the evening is destroyed as I struggle to pretend I am having a good time. The evening drags on as I try to look away and pretend I haven't seen her hand.

After the dinner, I offer, "Can we give you a lift home?" I feel it is unsafe for her to get a taxi home. She turns the offer down for no particular reason as we share awkward hugs and kisses on cheeks and bid farewell. With her now having left, the three of us make our way home in my car.

I cannot imagine what it must have been like for my children—especially my son, whose birthday it was—to see their mother leaving them. On a journey away to another home and life of which we knew very little at that stage.

Once back at home, I ask my children, "Did you notice the missing wedding band as well?"

"No, dad, we didn't," and once again, I drift further from happiness.

I am acutely aware of how this is affecting my children but struggle to keep my personal expression of grief away from them.

It is etched on my face. It shows in my eyes, and in my now buckling posture. It shows in my demeanour and my speech. Soul-destroying. I take the poison prescribed and go to bed still unaware of what route I am on.

A few weeks into my life of spousal isolation in the empty house, I receive a phone call from my mother-in-law, inviting me to have tea at her home. I am quite happy to do this and hope there would be some positive news to uplift me.

As conversations go, it is casual and friendly. She then gives me some advice on how I need to be strong, as Jackie respected strength.

I wonder how I am to be strong and try and win back the person who has destroyed my self-esteem and confidence?

Then, out of the blue, my mother-in-law says to me, "You do know she HAS left you?"

These words have never crossed my mind and once burnt into my soul, would never leave me again. It is brutally honest, and so painful. So, is that IT?

I stare at her aghast, not wanting to believe what I have just heard. Jackie must have told them things that she was reluctant or too afraid to tell me. I didn't want to hear those words, but how was I to make them go away?

I am still under the impression Jackie is away "working her mind out" or "working through this process" as she referred to it. With the salient point made very clear, I leave the home with the rain pouring and my spirits drowned a little more… It was the last time I ever went back to that home… another isolation complete!

AFRIKABURN AND CAROLINE

Jackie and I intermittently attempt to have lunches at Nicholas's cottage. It seems like a good reason at the time for me, as it offers some reconciliatory potential. Still, I think if we did this and I tried to work at it, then we have a chance to save the marriage, and in my mind, our family. The lunches feel like the most difficult dating game I have ever played. With the woman I am still married to...

Before one of the lunches, she calls me. "Please, Craig, when you come and visit, can you bring a bit of the rocket that's at home outside the front door?"

"Yes, sure, that will be no problem," is my response.

"That would be so kind," she says.

This basic charming request to me seems like a reconciliatory gesture. One that offers a glimmer of hope. It is something from home. Our home.

"Ah, she remembers."

So much that once again, I know we have hope for the marriage. I was clinging, again. I pluck a bunch of the rocket from the bush, place it into a small plastic bag, and make my way to the car for the lunch-of-hope.

"Are you prepared to go for couples counselling?" I ask, hopeful.

"That's probably a good idea," she responds.

We have hope. We cling. We grasp. Snatching at the butterflies that flit past us, temptingly just out of reach. Butterfly sans. Sadly, none of the butterflies settled for us.

THE COUPLE'S COUNSEL

Two cars park, one behind the other, under the huge shady trees outside the psychologist's rooms as the clouds threaten once again above. Meeting outside the main gate of the house, I bumble like a teenager through the 'do I hug her, kiss her on the cheek, kiss her on the lips, or just shake hands?' Walking in through the open door just as the previous client leaves, I wonder silently to myself, *what problem does that person have? Is it worse than mine? Is it solvable? Will he be coming here much longer? Will he be rescued by the professional ears that listen?*

Sitting down next to each other on the three-seater couch, I strategically move the tissue boxes around the table in front of us. You see, they were always going to be necessary that day as they would either dab away tears of joy, or mop up those that accompanied sadness.

The tissues waited, for now. I should have kept the whole bloody lot right there in my hands.

"So, how are things going?" asks the psychologist.

I enthusiastically respond, "Well, I think," as I recall how Jackie and I had gone out to lunch the Sunday prior to this counselling session. That specific day, I had bravely held her hand as we crossed the road, just like a grade-eight child, proudly getting to 'first base'. I had felt my heart skip a beat as that first-love feeling fluttered inside my tummy, like that of a love-sick teenager for a brief moment. I was protecting the lady I loved, and laying claim to the woman that was mine.

"Who could not like, Craig?" Jackie says. "Everyone likes Craig."

"But it is not the same."

"I do still love you, but not as a wife and partner anymore," she says, looking askance at me.

Jackie sits beside me on the couch and I look at her aghast. I had once, twenty-years prior to this day, drawn a picture of her from a photograph that had been taken for photo-shoot, and had given it to her as a birthday gift. The face she showed me that fateful day was the same oblique profile from that picture!

Short brown hair, lovely blue slanted eyes, high collar turned up, framing her neck. But the love is gone. Replaced by tears. Flowing. To me. From me.

Support from the counsellor stalls as I notice that even SHE is suppressing her tears. She had always believed that there was still hope for us, as she has known Jackie for several years, and had too believed the farce that had been presented in previous sessions. For in the end, that is what it was—a farce. It had been an ever-changing farcical story propping up the lie and stalling the inevitable demise of the relationship of our marriage, and it had all came tumbling down around us.

The counselling session now completed, I clear the table-full of tear-soaked, snotty tissues that lie scattered about, and walk her out of the psychologist's home and towards her car to say goodbye. I am not used to goodbyes. We have shared hundreds of "Cheers," "See you later," "Have a great day" and so on over the years, but never a "goodbye." Goodbyes seem too final and depressing. They signify an ending or permanence that we would rather avoid, and so replace them with a softer "farewell".

"Shit, no," even THAT sounds tragic.

We say goodbye to the psychologist and make a short pathway seem extremely long. It is the last time I consult that psychologist. Standing outside the driver's door of her car as Jackie sits in the front seat at the steering-wheel, I look at her questioningly. "Who are you going away with on the getaway?"

"Some friends," is the vague answer.

"And where are you going to?"

"To AfrikaBurn."

"What?"

This was possibly one of the most absurd moments in the demise of the marriage! AfrikaBurn is an artistic annual pilgrimage to the heart of the Karoo semi-desert. 'An official Burning Man regional event' according to the website advertisement.

People of all different ways of life congregate over a few days in an apparently spiritual celebration of art, sculpture, nudity, mirth, alcohol, and drug-taking. And some sobriety, I guess. You choose your vice, cause, and celebration, and go ahead in peace. As I understand everyone is accepted there in the name of freedom.

At the end of the celebrations, the artworks and sculptures are burnt in an orgy of fire and emotional purging. Jackie and I had never been to AfrikaBurn before, by mutual agreement. It just wasn't 'our thing'.

My sister, Paige and her husband, Brad had gone to AfrikaBurn a year prior to this and Jackie had made much mirth about why they would be doing this and why she, would NEVER DO THIS. I had agreed with her at the time. Yet, a few months later she was doing the same thing.

Choking down a glass of humility, I stop, not knowing whether to laugh, scream, or cry.

"You have to be joking?" My god, she is being incongruent again!

The rain is falling rather unforgivingly by now. Maudlin.

Fuck you both, it seems to say.

A kiss goodbye through the open window; forever hopeful that a gesture of love or affection will change her thoughts and intentions, bringing her bounding in slow-motion to the sound of violins out of the car and back to me. I will take her home and we will be one again.

THAT'S how it is supposed to end!

She sits behind the steering wheel of her car and I have mistakenly allowed myself another moment of hope. I am STILL chasing ghosts. Staring at her, I remove my wedding band and pass it across through the car window, saying "I think you should keep this for a while and give it back to me when you come home."

Awash with rain, the drops dilute my salty tears, hiding them from others as I slowly wade across the road to my car and leave. Having driven a mere two residential blocks away, I pull over to the curb and break down. I call her on the phone, sobbing, to ask, "Why do I always question my decisions, Jackie?"

"I need to see you now," I continue.

We don't. The rain pours as I sit in my car, not five hundred metres from the cottage she stays in.

Jackie says, "Maybe I SHOULD keep the wedding ring for a while."

I still hold some hope that I can get it back one day. She still has the ring.

CONFIRMATION TO A WEARY HEART AND SOUL

The loss or death of a spouse or partner is different to other losses, in the sense in that it literally changes every single thing in your world going forward.
When you spouse dies or leaves, the way you eat changes. The way you watch TV changes.
Your friend circle changes (or disappears entirely).
Your family dynamic/life changes.
Your financial status changes.
Your job situation changes.
It affects your self-worth.
Your self-esteem.
Your confidence.
Your rhythms.
The way you breathe.
Your mentality.
Your brain function. (Ever heard the term 'widow brain?' If you don't know what that is count yourself lucky.)
Your physical body.
Your hobbies and interests.
Your sense of security.

> Your sense of humour.
> Your sense of womanhood or manhood.
> EVERY. SINGLE.THING. CHANGES.
> You are handed a new life that you never asked for and that you don't particularly want.
> It is the hardest, most gut-wrenching, horrific, life-altering of things to live with.
>
> —(author unknown)

This reality starts to settle into my soul. It claws a giant hole in there and beds down to rot.

My beautiful friend, Caroline, had moved to the United Kingdom a few short years earlier to make use of the more efficient medical care system available in England. We had maintained a business relationship in the medical care field for over fifteen years, and I had walked many emotional paths with her and her family, including an emotionally abusive boyfriend and husband. We had spent many years and days supporting medical clients as business associates and even more hours drinking socially and chatting.

She had fought cancer on and off for at least fifteen of the twenty years I had known her, and the medical support in South Africa had waned substantially, especially if you were financially constrained.

She is one of the first people I call about my separation.

"Come to England and I can look after you as you

supported me whenever I was down."

I think she is serious, as most likely, she needs the emotional support of a friend. Her whole support group and family are still based in South Africa.

"Naturally, I can't. Firstly, I have business and family commitments and I have no British passport, Caroline," So, that is a non-starter.

A darker night falls when, during the evacuation from my home by my spouse, Lisa walks in with a sad look on her face.

"Dad, I have bad news, but Caroline died last night." She jumps right into it; no point mincing words.

"What?" I stare back, dumb-founded.

I don't need the message to be repeated.

"How?"

"I don't know, dad. Jamie (Caroline's daughter) called me and said she needed to let you know as you are an executor of the estate."

I had known that this was the case, as Caroline had asked me to be the executor a few years earlier; but for the life of me, I never thought my services would be needed this soon.

"Your timing is really shit, Caroline," I think, fully aware of the selfish sentiment.

I can't bring myself to call Jamie. I am so deeply soaked in shock, sadness, and anxiety, that my mind will not process and absorb the news. It is just too much to cope with, so I hide it from myself, tucking it away for another day.

The medication has destroyed all my emotions... No sadness. No crying. Nothing. Again.

I didn't make contact with Jamie for a whole year after the fact, as it was beyond my emotional capability then. Fortunately, a mutual friend was joint executor of the estate and brought the situation to conclusion.

A day or two after getting the news, I receive a WhatsApp message from Jackie with a photograph of a cross on some abandoned farm in the Karoo with the words "So sorry about Caroline." I am sure the intention is genuine but it falls on deaf ears.

She is on the way back from AfrikaBurn and a getaway with the new nameless friends that probably included Mark, although she never admits to it. I wish I had not received the message and picture—it seems so shallow to me and has lost all meaning over the hundreds of kilometres it has travelled. She was making a new life with others and really didn't appear to give a shit about those left behind in her wake. It was token emotion.

Human nature seems at times to have the ability of taking the 'final straw that breaks the camel's back' and turning it into 'water off the duck's back'. It is not a willing rejection of emotion, but rather a self-protection mechanism that says; you can't take any more of this, so I will put it aside for a while. Please make it back from the place you find yourself right now because I miss you; and then, when you are back from that place and can cope with what you have lost, I will address it with you again. Until then, I love you and please look after yourself.

Sincerely,

Your mind, body, and soul.

RIVERSIDE CLINIC

It is a Sunday morning a few weeks later, when Jackie comes to our home in Pine Avenue to remove some crockery and cutlery for her new rental cottage. My children have warned me not to be there, as I am not emotionally ready to witness this process of her packing and moving possessions out of our house.

"I don't think it's a good idea, dad," Lisa warns.

Stupidly, I don't listen to them. Not believing myself, I respond, "I'll be ok." I want to show strength.

From the moment she arrives, it is obvious that the distance between Jackie and I has widened to a chasm. This is one more shaving off of the veneer of happiness as well as the hope I had had, as through all this time I guess I had wished for something to change. To re-set. To go back to where we were, or where I thought we had been.

My good friend, Gavin, had said to me more than once, "Craig, are you sure you are not chasing ghosts?"

I was…

I was hankering after something that was gone and most likely lost forever. I am starting to look haggard and tired (which of course, I am). Jackie approaches me with tears in her eyes, putting her hands on my cheeks. I know she feels sorry, but I am not sure for whom. I feel even more sympathy for myself... misery loves company.

Plates are packed into boxes for her new living space at the cottage away from us. I stare, blankly. After a long discussion about the state I was in, we decide we are going to look at clinics to help me; as for damn sure, we both know I need some help. Even if it is just to teach me to learn to sleep again. But first, she will buy me lunch.

We drive to the Italian restaurant that we had habitually visited as a family, every Friday evening. It is a comfortable home-away-from-home and we are welcomed inside by the familiar waiters as they bring us the food and drinks we like.

The lunch is cordial and purposeful, but not comfortable by any means. The relationship has become more business-like. Smiles and familiar, affectionate touches have been replaced by serious discussions and a cold distance across a dinner table. Family and happy couple dinners are now definitely a thing of the past. A distant, hazy memory.

Once the lunch is over, we leave through the entrance at the front of the restaurant. As we pass the Chinese restaurant next door, our daughter, Lisa, and her boyfriend step out of it and into the daylight. Coincidentally, they have been there to get takeaways. Shocked by the sudden appearance of her dad and estranged mother, Lisa's face drops. To her, it must seem like an illusion. Her mother and father walking out of the homely restaurant AT THE SAME TIME!

Have we decided to make amends and try again? No. Lisa has not spoken to or seen her mother in weeks, as she is so very angry about what has been done that, she wanted no communication with her for a while. But here, life has forced an interaction upon her. What can she do but say, "Hi mom," give her a hug, and then move on? Jackie and I continue to the car, still a fractured couple.

The first exploratory visit is to Spiritual Retreat in Randburg. Spiritual Retreat is one of a chain of psychiatric recovery facilities in South Africa and this one is the first to come to mind as an option. It is the closest facility of its type to my home and thus also to my children and extended support group. This is my first time in any facility of this sort, including as a visitor.

We meet one of the administration staff who then proudly guides us through the facility. Our uncoordinated footsteps echo coldly down the vinyl floor hallway as we move from space to space. A room here with three beds crammed together accommodating three room-mates. A therapy group in a room adjacent to the eating hall presents ten or so patients of various ages, quietly discussing the task at hand. I feel so out of place; it's as though I am going back to school in a dream and am too old to be there.

A cold, shaded garden with a green swimming pool—left unattended and ignored—in the winter afternoon adds to the sadness. I will not be able to thrive here if I start out so down and negative.

The brief tour of the facility very quickly convinces me that this place is not for me. The thought of sharing a room with two other unknowns at the age of fifty-three is unfathomable.

We return to the car in the sunny car-park, and proceed to option number two. This facility is a 'country retreat' that one would only want to retreat FROM, in retrospect.

Riverside Clinic... ah how peaceful it sounds! It is a bit clinical (after all, it is a clinic with a twist); however, at the time of psychological desperation, it looks like a temporary Nirvana. I hope I will learn to sleep again.

Can they teach me? Can they medicate me into it? If only for a short time. Can they find me enough sleep to filter the haziness of exhaustion out of my body and then enable me to start thinking logically once again?

I don't pay much attention to the heavy security door as it clangs behind us as we move from the reception area again and towards the bedrooms and nurse's station.

"The gate is to keep people out, not in; so, don't be concerned," the nurse tries to lighten the mood with a grin.

It is a Sunday afternoon and some patients have visitors, which adds a veneer of comfort to the cold, clinical facility. It feels better than the first facility for sure, but it still reminds me of an old-school hostel.

Tired yellow face-brick walls with faded red corrugated iron roofing complete the image. The afternoon sun streams through one of the bedroom windows I look into, and I envisage myself reclining on the bed in the rays and healing. I must make a call and soon. I decide that I will take the two-week 'course' at this clinic, starting the very next day. It is not an exciting decision, but more like one of acceptance and hope. We drive back to my home with the decision made.

"Cheers, Jackie."

No kisses; no "I love you."

On my own again.

Take the medicine and go to bed.

THE TRIP DOWNHILL

A weekend bag packed to the brim with enthusiasm and hope accompanies me to the car on that Monday morning. I have enough clothes for a week or two, a flashlight in case the power runs out, and a chocolate bar for comfort. A book for the quiet, personal hours, and the regulation National Geographic rounds off the scheduled stay.

This should get me through until I see my babies again and take them back to safety with me.

My sisters assist in checking me into the facility. It is supposed to be for only fourteen days, which, even at the time, seems impossibly long!

Little do I know this is to be the precursor of bigger things to come.

Growth through depletion.

They show me to my room, and I glance at the doorway as a spectre of a human drifts dazedly past. He seems unaware of the people in the facility and the surroundings. They introduce him as my room-mate!

Visibly shocked by his appearance, I immediately start doubting my reasons for being there.

"Would I end up like that? Did the person arrive at the facility in that state?"

"Are you sure you still want to be here?" Kim has a cynical smirk on her face.

Doubting my decision, I respond, "Shit, I am not sure!"

"What happened to that chap?" I query from the admissions nurse.

"He responded really badly to Electro-Convulsive-Therapy and is under intensive observation."

With his visiting family holding out hope-beyond-hope for his recovery, he continues, apparently unaware of his whereabouts.

The cold room and vacant bed allocated to me seems strangely comforting on the first evening, as it holds out hope for sleep.

Lack of sleep is still driving the exhaustion and compounding my sadness.

My first night at Riverside Clinic includes a gentle introduction to my 'NEW' psychiatrist!

"Fuck, not another one," I think to myself.

It will have to be another process of relating my

sad tale...Another scraping of the partially-healed scab off the wound... Rubbing my nose in the rectum of psychiatry's bullshit...

I am so tired of repeating my story and issue, but must do it all over again for the umpteenth time, and ALL I want to do is get some sleep. I am convinced that good sleep will ease the sadness. The psychiatrists, of course, feel that an anti-depressant will assist with sleep.

"I actually want to cope without any medication," I explain.

"Just give me six weeks," she responds confidently.

"Six weeks!" I think...*that's 42 days, 1008 hours, 60 480 minutes! I need to be well NOW! I can't wait that long.*

The new psychiatrist takes me off the Remeron and replaces it with the Serlife (Sertraline or Zoloft is an SSRI) and Seroquel (Quetiapine an atypical antipsychotic which was prescribed as a 'mood stabiliser'). As I was not psychotic; this is known as off-label prescribing.

This process of moving a patient from one drug to another without weaning is known as 'Bridging' and is described by Holly Noble Myers (Director, State of North Carolina at the Coalition for Drug Awareness) as;

"... it is often used by doctors when a patient wants to wean off an antidepressant that has a short half-life. It can put a patient in danger of Serotonin Syndrome and may not prevent the withdrawal symptoms from the first antidepressant."

This is what they do; they listen to your sad story

and then give you pills. Cold turkey off the Remeron and straight into another drug of her choice. Hell, what do I know? They are apparently the professionals.

Twice a day at the allotted time, we as patients stand in a queue at the nurse's station to receive our daily 'bread' of prescribed medication. A small plastic container with our name handwritten on a little piece of paper is placed on the counter in front of the queue of hope and sadness. Accompanying the name tag inside the plastic cup is the bright pharmaceutical 'solution' to our problems. Bright orange, yellow, and green capsules make up our personal pharmaceutical fruit salad. To all the people there, the small plastic cup represents hope. It is a hint at the promise of recovery.

To the left of the medicine cups stands a tray with sandwiches cut into quarters and covered with a transparent cover to keep the flies off. The process starts with the eating of the sandwich quarter. This is to protect the stomach from the medicine to come (remember, no medicine on an empty stomach). The sandwich is then chased down with the medicine cocktail that is specific to the individual's prescription and affliction, and washed down with a small glass of water.

"This is so much like the Unholy Communion," I quip with a smile on my face.

We queue and shuffle forward on the psychiatric production line as the voice urges, "Next," whilst we hope for mental salvation; to be raptured from torment and anguish so-as to be delivered unto peaceful stability and everlasting happiness.

After the consumption of the Unholy Communion, each person strolls to different parts of the facility and groups together in patches of common interest as we wait for the medication to take hold and do its work. The smokers go outside for their nicotine fix, the non-smokers adjourn to the television room to watch some out-dated DVD, and yet others like me retreat into quiet, solitary isolation. With routine the order of the day, bed time is 21h00 and lights-out an hour later.

Night one and two entail my psychiatrist prescribing a sleeping agent injection in addition to the anti-depressants. The nurse on duty on the first night plunges the rather thick needle into my skinny arm as the natural place of application. This hurts like hell as the fluid is rather thick and appears to have a syrupy consistency (hence the thick needle). I wince with discomfort.

"Ouch, shit!" I tolerate it bravely as she slowly plunges the contents of the syringe into what is left of the muscle in my arm. I feel relieved afterwards as I have placed so much faith in the medical staff at the facility that I have little doubt I will sleep like a baby. I make my way to the bedroom and lie down, closing my eyes, all the while clinging onto hope.

To add insult to injury the 'angel of darkness' has prescribed some other shit that makes the floor look like my bed is floating on a sea of vinyl puke. It literally waves at me as I sit there lurching on the waves that are tossing my bed about the room. This feels good initially as it lulls me into a false sense of security and I feel relaxed at last. I seem to be able to think logically for that short while and try to write a to-do list for my immediate future ...

I will make peace with Jackie, sort out a divorce agreement, buy a new house that my children and I could move into, go back to work. Alternatively, I could complete a pilot licence and start flying; that was a career I have always wanted to pursue. (This was illogical as my eyes were way too unreliable for this option. It was merely drugged elation in retrospect).

I am led to believe the dose of the injection was strong enough to kill a horse, but apparently, it could not even give one very sad, desperately lovesick middle-aged white male from Africa more than four hours of nocturnal delirium!

Unfortunately, the drug's effect always lasts only about three to four hours until I feel it wearing off. This makes me even more desperate and afraid I will never find a solution or happiness.

The second evening, the nurses try another type of sleeping injection in the hope that THIS one will work better. I ask them to find another spot other than my rather bony arm.

They default to the butt cheek. I drop one side of my pants, exposing my right cheek and assume the position.

"Ouch," I mutter whilst screaming *fuck* in my head as they shove the bicycle-pump sized needle into my gluteus-not-so-maximus. This is as painful as the previous evening, and causes me to start doubting the capabilities of the nurses and the psychiatrist's abilities to prescribe effectively. I am disappointed to find the same marginal effect on my sleep with another dose of darkness lasting merely four hours and then once again a rapid awakening with a shock.

Tossing and turning for the rest of the night, dawn creeps up on me. As confused as I am, my mind never rests. There is just too much going on in my life to try and sort out. Things must be done in stages, but I don't know what the first step is. The exhaustion intensifies unforgivingly, adding to my anxiety.

Every day I wake up a bit earlier than the day before, with the noise of the road-works on-going at the highway from Krugersdorp to Pretoria and the damned construction vehicles beep, beep, beep, beeping ALL night long.

Adding insult to injury, I have the additional 'blessing' from the sky gods at Lanseria airport as they send the first 6 am flight to the place 'normal' people go to on their journey in their daily 'normal' life. The fear of not returning to a normal life is becoming a great concern as the days march on relentlessly.

It is day four or five after the 'angel of darkness' prescribed a new oral poison called Serlife, (another SSRI), much against my desire. Once again, as all the others caught in the 'system' do, I oblige and succumb as "the doctors know better than we do". So, as patients, we hand over our lives to them.

We do it all in good faith. As long as they are paid before we claim from medi-care.

Since the revelation of my marital demise had started to sink in, I had continuously lost weight. This had continued unabated for months and I had not managed to find a way to alleviate it. At the very least, it needed to stop; with a bit of luck, it would possibly start to move in the opposite direction so I could get my weight up to a healthy middle range.

"Doctor, please can you arrange for a more nutritional diet with more calories?"

"No problem. I will pass on the instruction to catering," she accommodates willingly.

With the nutritional instruction apparently being passed onto the catering staff, one would have assumed—in an expensive private recovery unit—that it would have been implemented.

The catering-staff are actually quite pleasant and efficient and always know everybody's names as well as the patients' culinary options—it is one of two choices anyway. Something like the 'chicken or beef' option offered by airlines the world over. The lunch option needs to be decided on during the morning breakfast and then the supper option at lunch time. If you happen to change your mind, well then, it is tough luck. You make your choice, so you now stick to it as it was planned for earlier on.

I find the staff very friendly, yet looking at their responsibilities over time, I realised that they were part of the munching mafia that forced the patients to eat even if they were not hungry. If the patients were not eating, then the catering staff would be obliged to let the medical staff know so that corrective steps could be taken.

Most of this followed a medical and psychological advisory pattern as it is symptomatic of people who are suffering from depression and the associated anxiety that they end up with some form of eating disorder.

HOWEVER, it is also a side effect of many psychiatrically prescribed drugs, including benzodiazepines, SSRIs and other anti-psychotics. Most of the medical leaflet inserts in the packages give side-effect warnings and possibilities, and a massive percentage state anorexia as a possible side-effect.

The anti-depressant I had been prescribed at the time, namely Serlife, is an SSRI. The pamphlet states under two categories, namely; *Metabolism and Nutrition Disorders and Psychiatric Disorders*, that Anorexia is a "common" side effect and Insomnia "very common".

And this for a patient who had come for treatment for insomnia which was leading to depression! So, it is there for all to see, provided by the pharmaceutical manufacturers themselves. Less common side-effects of Zoloft according to Drugs.com are:

"Aggressive reaction, breast tenderness or enlargement, confusion, convulsions, diarrhoea, drowsiness, dryness of the mouth, fast talking and excited feelings or actions that are out of control, fever, inability to sit still, increase in body movements, increased sweating, increased thirst, lack of energy, loss of bladder control, mood or behaviour changes, muscle spasm or jerking of all extremities, nosebleeds, overactive reflexes, racing heartbeat, red or purple spots on the skin, restlessness, shivering, skin rashes hives or itching, sudden loss of consciousness, unusual or sudden body or facial movements or postures,

unusual secretion of milk (in females), changes in vision, cloudy urine, constipation, increased appetite, difficult burning or painful urination, frequent urge to urinate, pain or tenderness around the eyes and cheekbones, agitation anxiety or nervousness, bladder pain etc."

So, don't worry, they've got this covered!

Just be aware of how your body is feeling!!

The question for patients is this: are they showing symptoms of anxiety and depression or are they presenting symptoms of the side-effects of the medication that they have been prescribed? Both are possible and both are applicable.

To top it all, when psychiatrists change a medical regime that is 'not working' they alter the prescription, very often changing the patient 'cold turkey' off the failed script, starting immediately with the new regime and prescription. The problem with this method is that, whilst the patient is being phased into the new drug 'attempt' (for that is what it is, merely an attempt) they have gone 'cold turkey' off the previous script. Now, as the patient has gone 'cold turkey' off one drug, he starts presenting withdrawal symptoms which may be interpreted as the original symptoms returning—namely anxiety, depression, anger, suicidal ideations etc. Our medical professionals then often re-prescribe medication for the side-effects of withdrawal from the medication they have taken the patients off of, instead of looking at all the possible reasons the patients may be presenting the symptoms.

These are often preceded by tolerance

withdrawals…the process of patients building up a tolerance to the medication prescribed by the medical 'professional' as their bodies naturally become used to the medication. The patient's tolerance builds up as the human body has no need to build its own form of support against the threat from its psychological weakness. In turn, the body finds the dose insufficient to support its new need. AND our doctors increase the dose and in so-doing, increase our reliance on the artificial solution.

It becomes a vicious cycle that, when needed, makes the titration process and weaning off the drug regime nigh impossible as the dosage has been progressively increased to an unimaginably high level. This is drug dependence, NOT drug abuse.

―― ―― ――

Standing facing the window, I wheel around as the door eases open. A young man accompanied by his conservative-looking mother enters the room. His arm extends as a book with a black cover thuds onto the desk. I glance down at it; *The Book of Mormon* is emblazoned across the front cover in cheap gold lettering.

Really? echoes through my mind.

My new roommate is a twenty-something Mormon with a drug problem! This should be interesting. He seems polite enough and introduces himself as he settles on the only other unoccupied bed closest to the door. Unpacking his bag, his mother leaves him to get on with his first day as I wait and watch the process.

The late afternoon passes by uneventfully until we have all showered, been medicated, and go to bed. Lights out.

"Kill! Kill! Give my knife! Give me my knife! Kill… Kill!" The words tear me from the rare moment of drugged sleep I had been enjoying.

"What the fuck is going on?"

There is no light in the room as my imagination plays games with my eyes searching for a shape confirming my imminent death. Is this child-of-Mormon going to hack me to bits or will I manage to survive the night?

There is no silhouette forming from the black ether, so I must assume he is still in bed and the threat to me is not imminent. I stare into the darkness in terrified silence as the demons in the Mormon's head toy with his sleeping mind, his voice growling incantations for what seems like an eternity. Slowly, they eventually slip away to taunt another's sanity as the shape on the other bed mumbles and slurs down to silence once again. There will be no more sleep for me until day-break.

The child-of-Mormon awakes the next day and shyly asks me, "Did anything happen last night?"

"No everything was fine," I lie, whilst later giving the full report to the nurse's station just in case the demons in his mind reside there permanently. Much to my relief, he is discharged and moved to another facility that day.

The days at Riverside Clinic drag on as one would expect. I have one continuous goal in mind and that is to try and learn to sleep, and then, once that is accomplished, leave—miraculously healed after only fourteen days of struggle.

Day five of my stay takes on a whole new significance as there is a dramatic shift in the way I feel. During supper, my appetite suddenly disappears completely. I have taken my choice of very moderate caterer's food and am sitting down with a group of temporary friends to have some company for the duration of the meal.

I start eating when an awareness envelopes me... almost instantaneously, I have no desire to finish my meal. It is not the specific meal that I am eating, but rather the desire for food itself. I do not want a replacement meal or anything fresher. I do not want hotter, sweeter, more bitter, saltier, meatier, vegetarian, or any other variant of culinary fascination.

I just don't want food. At all.

This is unusual for me, as I have already lost a massive amount of weight and am keen to pick it up again—never mind the fact that, from a health perspective, I NEED to pick it up anyway.

Along with the loss of appetite, I lose a willingness for anything at all. I struggle to see a way out of anything and everything. Visions of being in institutions forever, unemployed, and alone, overcome me. No children in the house, no wife, no future.

My positivity becomes a haze of negativity.

In truth, it is as if a cloud has descended over me with this darkness eventually solidifying into a brick wall a mile high and a million miles wide.

For me, there is no visible way out. Moving back

from the dining room and slowly shuffling towards the dormitory, I glance to my right at the sad, wintry, hazy, red sunset. My slow footsteps echo and clatter off the silent, face-brick walls as I make my way down to the dormitory for some disorganised time prior to the next sleep attempt.

Darkness has almost overwhelmed the sun, and the last cuddle of warmth strokes my shoulders as night closes the curtain on another day...

Another day has passed by with seemingly nothing achieved again. The daily commute from Pretoria and back from Krugersdorp continues on the highway adjacent to the clinic with arrogant disdain for the patients of Riverside Clinic. I stare at the highway and watch as the commuters' wheels roll on, each car's headlights urging the vehicle in front of it forwards. Again, I question myself...*Will I ever get back to that place...drive home?*

There is a rudimentary gym where the patients can exercise. A few of them do some early morning running. The gym seems to be rarely used and holds no appeal for me. It is too bland and merely reminds me of where I am physically and emotionally. There is no colour, and the basic barbells and dumbbells lay scattered around the cement room, disorganised and randomised, like my mind.

I had always been an active sportsman and would train almost every day when I had been in a normal family space. I watch as the other patients complete their exercises, returning from their sessions, bringing with them a disciplined sweat.

I am intrigued at how other people I had never known prior to this time are able to carry out as simple a thing as training for fitness. In the past, this would never have been an issue for me; yet now, it is case of how could I possibly raise myself to their level?

THEIR level? I was always way ahead of the 'mere mortals' in the past. My confidence is being replaced by self-deprecation as I decide I just wasn't good enough anymore.

The patients weren't allowed to leave the grounds at all unless the allocated psychiatrist had completed an authorised 'pass'. Had I insisted, I have no doubt I would have been issued one, for I had voluntarily been admitted to the facility. I somehow start to believe I am being detained against my will and that I will only be allowed to leave once I have successfully completed my two weeks' penance. This 'pass system' had not been imposed on me, since I had been conscripted to the South African army some thirty-five years prior and it makes me feel unwillingly incarcerated.

It is getting really cold now as winter digs its icy heels in and this only serves to reinforce that feeling of incarceration, as I had completed my army basic training (boot-camp) in the winter of 1982. The cold, dark, early mornings and afternoons feel all too familiar.

I had brought no gym clothing with me for the two-week stay, yet I nonetheless start to do a few laps of the clinic grounds, alternately walking and jogging within the confines of the boundary fence. The fence with the barbed-wire. The fence that keeps me in.

Slowly, on free afternoons, while doing my circuits around the dusty grounds, I pause briefly at the occasional tree and attempt a few pull-ups. I am weak as I haven't trained for months by now, but I try meekly. There is no real commitment as the process feels secondary in importance to my family's woes and my mental healing. All I am doing is creating sweaty, smelly clothes that I will wash at the end of the day and then struggle to get to dry in the cool shade of the washing lines.

I resort to wearing a set of clothes for two days in a row, and on occasion, will put on my still-damp socks in the hope that my body heat will dry them during the day. It is Hobson's choice of wet socks or stinky socks, and for me, wet for a while is a better option.

Fully aware of the clammy aroma I am now trailing behind me, I start caring less and less as the sadness and medication effects take hold. I sit in the therapy classes with other patients and am acutely aware of the funk I bring along. I feel slightly embarrassed, but I'm unwilling to do too much more to stop it. I could wash the clothes, but they won't dry timeously.

I need to see quick progress and it isn't happening at the desired pace. In fact, it isn't happening at all and I am actually regressing.

I watch as earlier entrants to Riverside Clinic graduate and are collected by their proud families. They have a family session where the concerns are raised, and the very well-prepared 'Relapse Prevention Plan' is presented to the family by the patient.

THIS plan is their individual and personal concept

on how they are going to avoid going back into the dark and possibly drugged place in their minds. They are packed with promises of a full life, and healing lays ahead for them. My sad decline hasn't even bottomed out at this point yet, I am envious of them and their comparative progress.

> "Depression relapse happens when a person slips back into depression during recovery from an earlier episode. Relapse is most likely to occur within two months of stopping treatment for a previous episode."
>
> —*American Psychiatric Association's practice guidelines.*

Once my running and exercise 'regime' has come to a standstill, I start strolling late in the afternoon on my own to the bottom of the grounds and sit on the dilapidated tennis court staring at the depressingly empty swimming pool next to it.

The pool must have been a part of the original home that occupied the old farm grounds that Riverside Clinic was built upon. It was fairly typical of the 1970s family in South Africa that had extra money to have a tennis court AND swimming pool on their property. With the passing of time and the growth and departure of the families, the need and costs of maintenance of these luxuries would render them unnecessary and they would inevitably fall into decay.

The last remains of the summer rainfall lie in all its fetid silence in the deep end of the decaying shell, which nurtures some green algae in its transformation to dark sludge.

Collectively, the tennis court and swimming pool are symbolic of the state I and other patients have fallen into. We are shattered and empty, with little chance of repair, needing a LOT of work with help from outside.

I pick up cracked chunks of the coloured all-weather tennis court from the ground and aimlessly toss them into the cavity below, all the time contemplating my fate and future.

Am I hoping that the broken pieces below my feet, once accumulated in the empty shell of the pool, will pile up and metamorphosise into my life's solution?

For a while, I make panicked, desperate telephone calls from this isolated base to my sisters and plead for advice. They try in frustration to assist me, but it is to no avail.

"Kim, how do I get out of this place?"

"Craig, what do you want to do?"

"I don't know, Kim."

I crunch dry leaves under my shoes as I pace the broken court, trying to get direction again from the advice I am being fed. Once the conversation is over, I depressingly and resignedly shuffle back up to the rooms and prepare for supper and the medication procession.

It is late one evening—and during a moment of much-needed sleep —when I awake in a panic! I feel a massive pressure over my chest cavity… I cannot breathe in at all. It is as if someone has placed a clamp on my chest and will not allow the free movement of air. Fearful and with much difficulty, I manage to get myself out of bed and stumble out of my room. I use the wall as support as I make my gasping way to the nurse's station. It feels like an eternity as the breathless twenty-meters of dark, cool passage wall pass by under my hands.

"Help!" I wheeze, terrified.

The nurses on night duty stare at me wide-eyed, asking, "What's the matter?"

I genuinely think I am having a heart-attack and have moments left to live. Somehow, I manage to describe the symptoms and they casually say, "It is a panic attack" and that I should try and calm down... They will give me another pill for this.

I am prescribed Pur Bloka, a beta blocker that calms the heart-rate and in turn is meant to calm one down and reduce the effects of the panic attack.

ANOTHER DAMN DRUG! is how I feel, but initially, we go with the advice of the medical facilitators.

ELECTRO-CONVULSIVE THERAPY

During one of the latter consultations of psychiatry, my 'angel of darkness' casually asks me, "Have you ever considered ECT?"

"What is that?" I enquire.

'Electro-Convulsive-Therapy' she quickly translates from the abbreviation for me in response to my quizzical look. I have never heard of this term, but once it has been explained to me, I recall scenes from films of people with electrodes taped to their heads, biting on a piece of wood whilst having the bejeezus knocked out of their brains—all in the name of psychiatric medicine.

Mayoclinic.org describes ECT as *"a procedure done under general anaesthesia, in which small electric currents are passed through the brain, intentionally triggering a brief seizure. ECT seems to cause changes in the brain chemistry that can quickly reverse symptoms of certain mental health conditions"*.

"It certainly speeds up the process," her explanation continues.

Desperate for a quick solution to my quandary, and after having the process and all its 'benefits' explained to me, I seriously consider having it done. This is disturbing to the casual observer, but according to conventional medicine, it has some success (assuming you believe psychiatry is conventional medicine). Statistical success will vary depending on who the doctor is, of course.

"Um, Natasha. You are having ECT, aren't you?" cautiously and apologetically I broach the question with another patient I have befriended.

"Yes, I am. Why do you ask?"

"My doctor suggested it and I wondered what it was like and how it made you feel. Does it work?"

This lady had lost her mother and sister to cancer all within a two-month period and is struggling with depression because of these tragedies.

"I have had it done a few times and I think it works,"

she says quietly.

I also discuss it with several of the other dazed, temporary zombies wafting about the facility who have had this procedure performed before to get some clarity to assist me in making the decision. They are all generally quite positive about the success of the procedure, but warn of the intense headaches that occur immediately after the shock treatment. Of all the people in the world, I am searching for advice from psychologically disturbed, depressed people like myself!

The head nurse on duty suggests, "Why don't you watch the clinic-provided video recording for all the relevant information on the procedure?" I don't bother, having heard enough from the people who had undergone the procedure and just want to get better, and quickly.

Shortly after this, it suddenly strikes me that a professional specialist, a psychiatrist, had asked her patient if he has ever considered having an operation performed? Surely, this is the last thing that should be attempted, and shouldn't THEY be telling ME what I need?

Riverside Clinic, in retrospect, must have had at least six ECT patients per day, if my estimation is correct. The medical staff there seemed to do it like dishing out toffees. The patients would miss breakfast as a pre-operative norm, and then come drifting through later in the day with the post-shock vagueness of temporary memory loss that is associated with ECT. This for me, is possibly the only deterrent as the question naturally is, "Is it really only temporary memory loss?" The physical pain I can cope with.

Some complain of headaches and others have very sore jaw muscles from the electrode-induced spams that cause the mandible to bite down. Some of the patients have minor bruising from where the electrodes have touched their temples and passed the electric shocks through to the relevant lobe in their brains. They need to do this five times within a few days to complete a treatment cycle. Unfortunately, one often needs "maintenance treatments" every six months or so. It is NOT a quick fix.

It is all in good faith though. They trust the doctors. It was too extreme, but I was STILL considering it. This was being sold to me as a quick-fix to healing!

Once this treatment option had been discussed with other medical professionals post my depression, the response had been that the procedure seemed to be an absolute last resort.

It was applied less by medical professionals in other places and countries.

Meanwhile my sleep has not improved at all. The medication at night gives me a temporary reprieve from the reality of my pending life's change; however, every morning before the early plane leaves the nearby airport, I awaken with the same feeling of loss of direction and hope. This happens earlier and earlier as my body rapidly reaches dosage tolerance and the effects of the drugs wear off quicker as my body becomes used to the dose.

As a result of the tolerance, my 'angel of darkness'

decides to double up my dose of Serlife. I find the name 'Serlife' rather ironic, because I feel increasingly like I am dying than living.

Where is the logic in this?

A medicine is not working, so let us INCREASE the dose and see what happens! Let's increase the poison as we search for a solution. As a medicated patient, one goes with the flow, as the thought of starting a new alternate drug regime seems more daunting than staying on the poison prescribed and waiting for positive results. This is because the drugs take two to four weeks to start working; and as I mentioned before, we as patients, are struggling to survive one day at a time.

So, six weeks feels like a lifetime of purgatory as we wait for our medical salvation. Yet unknowingly, many of us have already passed from purgatory and into hell, from where many never return. You wait as the Sword of Damocles hangs over your head, hoping that the statistics favour you today. As a result of this, we listen to our 'angels of darkness' and swallow the drugs, chased down with a massive dose of hope.

A day or so after this recent dosage increase, I start to feel the neurosis grow every moment and every day. I want to have visitors, but at the same time, can't cope with the interaction. I stop calling anyone on the phone at this time, and stop writing as well. I can't read—because I lack both the desire and the ability. I can't concentrate in any of the classes, and I struggle to rationalise. Doing basic tasks such as placing things in order of preference or priority become a challenge.

Decision-making becomes impossible, and my anxiety grows disproportionately. This extends even to making a decision between the two options of main course we have for lunch or supper each day. I am concerned about my children, but don't want to see them.

"Dad, do you want us to visit?"

"No, don't worry Lisa. It will be OK," I lie.

I am failing, mentally.

Physically.

Physiologically.

As a father.

As a man.

As a human being.

Having been a high-functioning individual, I am losing my functionality and my self-confidence has been summarily shattered. I am literally having the life poisoned out of me.

AND I feel I can't control it at all.

Through all my months between happiness and depression, I was ALWAYS aware of what was happening to me and around me, yet I had lost all control on how to handle it.

I am lost inside my head, tied up within my mind, multitudinous thoughts rattling around in my cranium. Like a pinball trying to find its way out and, in the process, trying to avoid the 'tilt button'.

Keep on pressing the 'flipper' at the right time, but take care not to shake the machine too hard in case it just switches off for good. I came very close to understanding what Stephen Hawkins must have felt like trapped in a malfunctioning body, with a fully aware mind. The difference between me and Stephen Hawkins, other than the obvious, was that I also had less control of my mind and was acutely aware of this. The medicine had started to take control, and not in a positive way. Spontaneity. Stopped.

JACKIE'S VISIT

My sister, Kim, had been visiting me for support as she felt I had been abandoned to this facility by my wife, even though I had agreed to the proposed therapies and facility and had volunteered for admission.

It is late afternoon at Riverside Clinic and we are sitting outside in the warm autumn sun chatting in general, when I notice the expression on my sister's face suddenly change. It moves from genuine concern to abject anger and disgust. I am confused about what I have possibly said until I see that her eyes are not directed at me, but instead past my face and up the stairwell behind. Glancing furtively over my shoulder, I see Jackie walking down the stairs in our direction. Her walking pace drops off markedly and becomes calculated and cautious as she locks eyes with Kim. It is too late now for her to turn around and retreat. This will show weakness and defeat, an admission she would never allow. This is not a good mix in this environment at all. It is oil and water with the oil about to ignite.

They greet each other curtly and the atmosphere

turns icy cold. The familiar family hugs and kisses of the past have long gone. These are two people in my family that had learnt to like each other and had mixed well for many years, but the rapid disappearance of Jackie from the home and from contact with my side of the family, has destroyed any semblance of love.

I am initially at a loss for words, but eventually stutter a greeting as I move to hug Jackie. Courtesy is still ingrained somewhere in my tortured soul. Kim, however, is NOT at a loss for words at all. "What the fuck are you doing here?" she growls.

There is no response from Jackie. She knows she is in shit-street and has walked herself right into the danger zone. A stilted silence follows and then…

"It's because of YOU that he's in this place!" Kim snaps.

Jackie has nothing to say in response to this. She merely stares at Kim emptily in return as she hands some documents that were clutched in her hand to me. They are the offer-to-purchase forms from the estate agent. Our house has been sold!

Behind the scenes, the psychologist at Riverside Clinic had apparently warned Jackie not to broach the subject of the home at this stage as I couldn't handle any more stress, but she ignored the request.

With the house sold (admittedly at a good price), it is now up to me to sign the acceptance or not. I know the sale is necessary, but the timing is so badly chosen that I cannot make a call. I am in a recuperative psychiatric facility and my estranged wife brings me the documents showing I am about to be without a home.

After a brief, stilted conversation Kim blurts out, "Tell him you are not coming back to him. Tell him you have left him!"

I hate to hear the words and block my ears like a child, mumbling, "No, don't say that."

It is true, but I can't cope with the truth. I was to repeat that sentiment and response to the in-house psychologist later in the week when she broached the subject of an 'affair' and 'separation'. The words were still too hard for me to hear and I preferred to banish them from my head. I could not and would not let them in. I needed to live in denial for now so as to crawl through the thorn-bushes of reality and find my own way out, scratched and bleeding.

Kim repeats the question to Jackie several times, but it does not bring forth the words that need to be said. Does she really think that the words can do MORE damage than her actions have already done?

Jackie is forced to leave with the unsigned documents in hand; she would later pass them on to other members of my family to gently coerce me to sign.

"Well, they can look after you now," is the parting shot from Jackie, insinuating the responsibility of my situation is to be handled by my direct family from hereon in. She is fobbing me off with disdain. It IS my fault, of course, that I am in this bad space. Remember, I have choices.

The twitches I started displaying that day, in retrospect, indicated to me that hyper-vigilance was starting to set in.

I suspiciously dart a glance over my shoulder at any quick movement as if my security has been compromised. I keep looking at the security cameras that covered the entrance of the residential section of Riverside Clinic, and then shuffle inside to look at the screen to see the other side.

> "Serlife, an SSRI, has been known to cause a side effect called 'hyper-vigilance' and is described as follows "...abnormally increased arousal, a high responsiveness to stimuli and a constant scanning of the environment for perceived threats. This symptom is also associated with Serotonin syndrome, a potentially life-threatening disease."
>
> —*Miller-Keane Encyclopaedia and Dictionary of Medicine, Nursing and Allied Health, Seventh Edition*

A week passes by quickly as I wait and hope for improvement. This is to no avail, and I keep feeling worse. Sleep doesn't improve.

Another panic attack on the way to breakfast sees me trying to settle down in a separate nursing room with Pur Bloka being fed to me to calm my heart rate. I spend the rest of the morning in the emergency room trying to 'breathe deeply and calm down' as instructed.

A weekend passes with a visitor's day that sees my closest friends and family visiting. They have arranged a picnic in the gardens for me, and we clumsily worked through the two hours together as they tried to lighten the burden for me. The awkwardness about me is picking up and is clearly evident to them. Once visitor's time is up, everyone goes back home, leaving me alone with the post-visit blues.

Later in the second week of my stay, my sisters get wind of my irrational consideration to have ECT. I vacillate between desperate calls to them and my original clinical psychologist, in whom I still have immense trust. I keep them on the phone for over an hour and talk in circles, looking for a solution and a decision or direction forward. I have lost all ability in making decisions, including those related to my health.

Through all this time, though, I always voiced my concern about taking too many drugs. I was against it, but if it worked, I was prepared to try. However, I felt the medication also played a part in my feeling so bad.

As for psychiatrists, I'd never had the need to consult with one prior to this event in my life, and certainly, I didn't have a clue as to how passionate and committed they are to giving you a pill to sort out the 'problem'.

Whilst at Riverside Clinic, I ask to have another psychiatrist allocated to me as I am struggling to identify with mine. I feel she was too quick to medicate and I want to get off drug therapy. The management staff chat to the alternate psychiatrist and the feedback to me later is, "Well if he (Craig) feels I am not going to medicate him then he can forget about it!"

Well, that pisses on my battery in a big way! It

short-circuits my desire for a quick fix.

As a side-bar, this doctor who insists on medication and who has rejected my request is one of the psychiatrists who is a major proponent for ECT for his patients. He is there early every morning to shock the patients out of their minds and the medical aid companies from their funds. With this wave of the hand from the other doctor, for now, I am forced to stay with my angel of darkness.

> "Most people are under the misconception that an appointment with a psychiatrist will involve counselling, probing questions and digging into the psychological meanings of one's distress," wrote psychiatrist Daniel Carlat of the Tufts University School of Medicine. "But the psychiatrist as psychotherapist is an endangered species." Carlat goes on to offer this frank observation about what has happened to the profession in The United States: "Doing psychotherapy doesn't pay enough. I can see three or four patients per hour if I focus on medications... but only one patient in that time period if I do therapy. The income differential is a powerful incentive to drop therapy from our repertoire of skills, and psychiatrists have generally followed the money."
>
> —*Extract from* The Drugs That Changed Our Minds *by Lauren Slater*

During the full year of my consultations and sitting in three different psychiatrists' consulting rooms, I was not once offered any counselling by them; yet, the prescription book was hauled out on every occasion. The average consultation lasted twenty minutes and I was charged at the average rate of R 2000 (US$ 200). One specific psychiatric practice would only take cash up-front. I suspect in the amoral manoeuvre to dodge the tax-man.

THE NOT-SO-GREAT ESCAPE

Without my knowledge, my sisters had decided in a caucus of ladies from the Dawtrey clan to haul me out of the clinic. My decision to have ECT done is a bad idea and, "Craig can't make sensible decisions." They were correct.

Meanwhile, my soon-to-be ex-wife and her side of the family were encouraging this radical treatment as a possible remedy. They also want a quick solution as "this has been going on for six months already."

I am scheduled for my first ECT treatment the next morning, a Friday. The clinic has received pre-approval for the procedure from the medical aid, justified and motivated by the psychiatrist at Riverside Clinic, so payment is guaranteed.

That Thursday evening, Kim calls me and asks if I want her to collect me and take me out of the clinic. Typically, I want to leave, but I've been to-and-fro between going and staying. Fortunately for me, she insists on coming to collect me and take me home as I otherwise would still have been debating the issue in my head.

She arrives that night as I pack my bags and have the relevant forms signed by the psychiatrist, allowing me to be discharged. The psychiatrist signs the forms with a gentle smile and, at Kim's suggestion, encourages a recuperative trip to the seaside.

We walk to the car-park that early evening, dragging my suit-case crammed with dirty clothes behind me. The sky is clear and the moon waxing towards full. I am hopeful, for a change.

One of the other female patients who managed to befriend me, accompanies us to the car. It amazes me how much support sufferers give to others in the same predicament as themselves. They want others to succeed, and if there is some visible success, then there MUST be hope for themselves.

THE KRUGERSDORP STAY

We are not ten minutes into the drive when I start to doubt my decision to leave Riverside Clinic. I am out of ANOTHER comfort zone. This is typical at the time, as I really can't make up my mind about anything and it is becoming worse every day. Despite my confused objections and comments about whether I have done the correct thing or not, we stick on course to my mother's home in a wintry Krugersdorp.

The dark night clings selfishly to the home as I enter. The once familiar sounds and smells of the house are now almost alien to me. It is almost unrecognisable; everything feels different. It feels hazy, dream-like.

My mother and sister try to make me feel comfortable by organising supper, running a bath, and helping me to feel relaxed and welcome, yet I still feel unsettled—guilty. The indulgence feels wrong and undeserved!

In fact, I think the guilt I felt for having left the clinic early, not going to my home where my children were, not working, and finally, just being helpless, had become overwhelming. I have never been this afraid and still don't know why.

For the next few months, every time I hear the phone ring, I am neurotically startled and worry about who it might be and what it is about. Trying to listen in to the conversations to see if I could work out what they are talking about, I start trying to look at every caller's details that have been corresponding with my mother. In my mind, every call is ALL about me.

Who was that? What did they say? Who is arriving at the gate? What did they want? As the hyper-vigilance worsens, my neurosis becomes overwhelming and affects everybody else as well; but once again, I feel I cannot control it.

At Riverside Clinic, we had been lectured about what foods and drinks to avoid due to our 'illness' and I started fixating on this advice, carrying this information out of Riverside Clinic and with me through the whole time I was in recovery. It continued to the point where I wouldn't eat or drink certain things in case it affected my sleep or resulted in a relapse (not that I had worked through this initial bout of depression yet, anyway).

~ No chocolate, as it has sugar and is a temporary upper that will spike your sugar level.
~ No junk food, as it also tends to spike your sugar levels.
~ No coffee and no tea, as it contains caffeine and this is a stimulant that can conflict with your medication.
~ No fizzy drinks.

- Be careful of fruit juices as they are high in sugar, which is a stimulant.
- No vitamins as this can affect your medication.
- No homeopathic medicine without the approval of the psychiatrist.
- No alcohol at all, as this is just not a good idea. Personally, I think I should have stayed off the anti-depressants and got drunk for a few months. Perhaps, when the hangovers ended, the pain might have subsided. At least, I knew how to handle a hangover, but THIS feeling of helplessness on drugs was beyond comprehension.
- Wake up at the same time every day and go to bed at the same time each evening.
- Don't exercise less than three hours before going to bed, as you might be too alert and mentally stimulated.
- Don't read in bed as bed is only for sleep and sex, this from the psychiatrist, and I was not being spoilt by any of these experiences, anyway! In fact, this specific psychiatrist humorously informed me after prescribing me Remeron that a potential side-effect was a two-hour erection! Though she "had never experienced this" herself. I almost saw the funny side. A two-hour erection at this stage of my life would have been an immense waste of time (but I am sure I could at least have made some money from it.)

- No television, iPads, or iPhones after 8 pm as blue screens over-stimulate the mind.
- No blue light.
- No bright light.
- No loud music.
- No living.
- And please, whilst you are at it, don't over-fixate and don't ruminate!

Jeez!

- Lastly, don't forget to take your poison at the same time each morning and night and not on an empty stomach—phew!

I was so glad I had nothing to worry about. So, I worried about it all. All the time. I wanted SO to eat, but stopped myself.

In the process, I doubted the value of the medication as I had started to suspect this was what was turning me into a fruit-cake. The SSRI medication, Serlife, was a brand similar to Zoloft, which I had been taken off before as I had reacted to it so badly in the past. The drug exacerbated all my depressive symptoms.

I knew I reacted badly to it, but did not draw a parallel between the two product names, otherwise I believe I would have refused to take it. This dose had been doubled up by now, as I had been on the initial dose for over five days and it was the prescribed procedure, so I had reluctantly complied.

Serlife was only one of my morning drugs as there had been a recent addition, called Pur Bloka. (Propranolol Hydrochloride is a beta blocker and used for tremor, chest pain, heart rhythm disorders, elevated blood pressure heart attack and other conditions).

This was to calm my heart, so I would stop having panic attacks and to lower my blood pressure.

What did I do? I stopped taking my blood pressure medication with this regime in the morning as the pill cocktail was starting to worry the living daylights out of me. Surely, I didn't need TWO pills for the high blood pressure? There was just too much medication on my plate.

> "Robert Whitaker, a finalist for the Pulitzer prize for public service journalism and a Polk award winner for his writing on medicine and science, proposes another scenario, which is that serotonin boosters, rather than treating a chemical imbalance, may instead be causing one. For starters, despite drug company advertisements and the prevailing 'neuro-speak,' there is, as we've seen, little evidence that mental illness is the result of a chemical imbalance. Scientists have searched and searched for evidence of this imbalance and have not been able to find it. Perhaps more to the point, when researchers have compared serotonin levels in depressed versus non-depressed subjects, they have found that the happy subjects do not necessarily have more serotonin than their depressed counterparts.

"In fact, sometimes the happy subjects have less serotonin than the depressed subjects.

"The results of these studies and others like them have turned psychiatry's dominant narrative of mental illness on its head. After all if there is no proof that a depressed person has a chemical imbalance, and you choose nevertheless to put that person on a medication that will alter neurotransmitter levels in his or her brain, then in effect you are causing chemical imbalance rather than curing one.

"Whitaker's main point was that we are subjecting millions of brains to drugs that change natural neurotransmission, sometimes radically, disturbing and upsetting the complex interplay within our heads, clogging neural pathways with excess chemicals and sometimes causing the entire brain, which is intricately interlinked, to malfunction in ways we do not yet understand. An un-medicated depressed patient does not have a known chemical imbalance in his brain, but once he ingests Fluoxetine (another SSRI), he will. The drug crosses the blood-brain barrier and gets to work, jamming serotonin in the synaptic cleft. Whitaker explains the result this way: 'several weeks later the serotonergic pathway is operating in a decidedly abnormal manner. The presynaptic neuron is putting out more serotonin than usual. Its serotonin uptake

> channels are blocked by the drug. The system's feedback loop is partially disabled.
>
> "The postsynaptic neurons are desensitised to serotonin. Mechanically speaking, the serotonergic system is now rather 'mucked up'.
>
> "As far as Whitaker, Glenmullen and other critics are concerned, the bewildering rise in mental illness is not due to social pressures but to the fact that so many people are drugged on serotonin boosters among other psychiatric medications and are therefore walking around with abnormal brain functioning that, in the long term, exacerbates the very symptoms the drugs are trying to treat. In other words, our antidepressants are making us increasingly depressed; thus, we turn to them still more keenly, upping the dose, which causes still more neural perturbations and abnormal functioning, and so we go around and round, down and down."
>
> —*Extract from The Drugs That Changed Our Minds by Lauren Slater*

I felt those changes and at no stage on Serlife did I ever feel it was helping. For me, it was a continual slide downwards in my feeling of wellbeing.

AT MY MOTHER'S HOME

I am sitting in the kitchen at supper time with my sister Kim, her two boys, and my mother. They are all waiting in frustrated anticipation for me to take my medicine so we could all could go to bed. Once again, the medicine will not pass my lips. The drugged anxiety convinces me that this is a side-effect of the drug combination as I have not felt this unwell since I started this regime. I start the day with a beta blocker and Serlife in the morning, followed by Mirtazapine and Stilnox at night.

> "A Mirtazapine drug may increase Serotonin and rarely cause a very serious condition called Serotonin Syndrome/toxicity. This is an SNRI (serotonin and Norepinephrine Reuptake Inhibitor) which works in a similar way to SSRIs. The risk increases when used with other drugs that increase serotonin..."
>
> —*Extract from WebMD*

Afraid that NOT taking them was a bad decision, I eventually take them late at night for a temporary, forgiving reprieve from the dark place I am in as the evening drugs take hold.

I was now prescribed an SSRI, a benzodiazepine, and an SNRI at the same time. I embrace a beautiful, yet all-too-short lift into happiness and logical thinking with relief and glee. Temporary clarity finds me in my sister's room where we chat animatedly as we drink tea and eat carrot cake.

We discuss the merits of being on medication and debate the down-side. We discuss how we should take two weeks and go to the ocean and enjoy the beach and some 'vitamin sea'. The plan is to drive to Kei Mouth in the Eastern Cape the very next Wednesday, go cold turkey off all the drugs, and hope that the alternate therapy of ocean air in my lungs and beach sand under my bare feet might make the difference.

After a few short hours, and just as I feel I am making a breakthrough, the curtain drops down over my happiness as the lucidity and the cold feeling of sadness envelop my whole being once again.

My family, who were with me during these times—both at my mother's home and then back at my house with my children—when this happened, saw the happiness drain from me. I would watch my daughter's face lose its brief glimpse of relief as she descended the sad steps with me, if only for a while. This destroys me further, as I can see the desperation in my family's faces, but still cannot control it.

Staring at the Stilnox (Zolpidem or Ambien are other brand names) sleeping pill that has been added to the mix—and not wanting to take it—I start resisting sleep. If I choose to take it, it works like a charm for a few hours as it knocks me out, but I awake with a jolt and am still in hell in my head with the same troubles I had left behind a few short hours ago.

Most of these sleeping pills are hypnotics and are highly addictive (another reason, I suspect, that the 'professionals' discourage patients from reading the inserts and warnings). Once I had been made aware that many of these drugs were so addictive—and really were not sleeping pills but hypnotics—I tried to manage the use of them attempting to reduce dosages or self-medicate. This was also not a good idea, but at this point I had in the region of six different types of pills prescribed and was feeling worse-for-wear, and had to take various doses three times a day. Most antidepressants raise the amount of Cortisol in the body and as a result can act as a stimulant.

I was on a benzodiazepine sleeping pill for sleep, and an antidepressant that was likely raising my Cortisol level and retarding my sleep. It feels as though my whole day and life is being dictated to by a drug regime and I am not living an even moderately full life. My weight continues to drop, bottoming out at seventy kilograms, having lost about 25% of my body weight. I don't want to bring myself to eat, yet, still feel hungry. So, having an enquiring mind, I check the insert for many of these drugs, only to find out that one of the side effects is a very high incidence of anorexia for patients! Surprise, surprise!

I have NEVER had any issues with food and am one of the few people in the universe that thinks that even Brussels sprouts are tasty! Considering that a patient shouldn't take medication on an empty stomach, this is swiftly followed by a resistance to me taking the medicine. It becomes one vicious cycle of daily and nightly toiling with myself and my family; I am fully aware that what I am doing is wrong, but still unable to alter my actions. I constantly feel drugged and continuously voice this to all the professionals when explaining my reluctance to taking the meds.

On occasion, my sister—in her frustration, along with her previous experience as a nurse—fools me by placing a pill in my food and then forces me to take the food, like a dog or naughty child, which is exactly how I started to act. I eventually comply as even I can see the obtuse side of what is going on through my haze, and give in only to be angry with her for fooling me.

In anger and frustration, I sit up in the kitchen after everyone else had gone to bed and watch as a small dormouse sneaks its way into the kitchen. It peers cautiously in my direction; then, with more confidence, slowly makes its way toward the dog food. Watching it as it takes small bites of the food, I hear the amplified sounds of its crunching, eating, and scratching as it digs its way through the dog food packet. I make no effort in stopping it, being rather more fascinated with its behaviour. It is brave. Even a small mouse finds no threat in me anymore.

> "I'm a brave, brave mouse
> I go marching through the house
> And I'm not afraid of anything"

I recall the song from my nursery school,

> "and what about the giant man in the corner?"
> "Well... no not even him, he's just a depressed, medicated giant anyway."

On every forty-eight-hour cycle, I avoid sleep as I don't want to take the sleeping pills. Occasionally, at three in the morning, Kim comes into the room. Waking up, she sees my light on and frustratedly walks into the room to ask, "Craig, are you still awake?"

"Yes." Of course, I am still awake.

"Take the damn pill and go to sleep." After this intervention, I agree to do so. Feeling severely reprimanded, it is of course far too late in the night to take a sleeping pill, but what the hell, at least I might sleep for a while.

I stop talking… literally. My mouth closes off to all communion and communication as a symptom of my mind shutting down. My voice fades from proud and deep to an asthmatic wheeze, and then eventually, disappears completely. Staring and not talking. It amazes me that a lack of use can destroy the voice so quickly. It is a muscle after all.

One freezing night, I stay up in bed, my foot tapping restlessly for hours as I concoct a catastrophic situation that strikes terror into me: Because I have left Riverside Clinic before the end of the fourteen day stay—and as a result have "Failed to Complete" the treatment—the medical aid will not cover the bills. Because they will not cover the bills, I will be financially liable. As I am liable and have been off work, I cannot receive my wages. As I will not receive my money, I will be sued by the medical aid and my membership summarily terminated. If the membership is terminated, then my children and I would be vulnerable, which will make me a bad father. My debit orders will all be returned unpaid, and as I can't pay the medical aid, the police will come and arrest me.

My car will be repossessed as well. So, I don't sleep. I interpret every siren I hear in Krugersdorp, as the police coming for me. Be still, my mind, please! I am catastrophising and irrationally view every situation in a much worse light than it actually is.

> "Catastrophising can generally take two different forms: making a catastrophe out of a current situation, and imagining a catastrophe out of a future situation."
>
> —Psychcentral.com

The first weekend after my not-so-great escape from Riverside Clinic, my family has arranged for me to have a session of reflexology—that lovely alternative, pampering foot massage therapy many people enjoy. The process starts with them trying to coerce me into the car. Insanity! Was this possibly an agoraphobic side-effect of the medicine?

> "Agoraphobia is an anxiety disorder characterised by symptoms of anxiety in situations where the person perceives their environment to be unsafe with no easy way to escape. These situations may include open spaces, public transport, shopping centres, or simply being outside their home... and might result in a panic attack."
>
> —Wikipedia

This should be an easy, normal activity, but the anxiety is overwhelming and it is becoming worse every day. Once they have me in the car and I have fidgeted and bumbled my way on the way there I, like a child, follow my mother into the rooms. I keep a drug-induced vow of silence throughout the therapy. The hyper-sensitivity of all my nerves makes the therapeutic effect too intense, and I don't enjoy the experience at all. I pretend politely to appreciate the gesture and flash a fake smile at the therapist as we leave.

The slow traffic leads us toward the highway as we make our way homeward. The whispering tyres grind discarded gravel, guiding the car off the side road and onto the highway.

Picking up speed as the scenery whips by, a desperate hand edges toward and then clutches the cold metal door-handle. A locked door temporarily stalls the person in the passenger seat. Why would I be tugging at it? Death is not an option! The rushing tar below will injure and possibly maim, but I don't want either. All that is needed is happiness again. The two hands unbuckle the seatbelt in a failed attempt to convince my mother there is nothing untoward intended. "What are you doing?"

Suicidal ideations aside, and driven by drugged side-effects, I resist the illogical urge to jump, knowing at heart it is wrong, cruel, and not wanted. The car slows as the door closes once again, and the passenger buckles up. There is light at the end of this road. Try and find it.

A conundrum if ever there was. As professionals tell the patients, "Don't read the information leaflet inserts in the medication packages." I suspect they say that for a damn good reason; it is because the potential side effects are so wide and all-encompassing and affect such a massive percentage of the 'subjects' that everyone would question, debate, and refuse the medication, and this would dilute the validity of the whole profession.

> "Treating depression with antidepressants may improve the condition, but may increase the risk of suicide."
>
> —*Drugwatch.com*
>
> "A clinical trial conducted by the FDA showed that the rate of suicidal thinking (ideations) doubled for patients taking SSRIs compared to those assigned to receive a placebo."
>
> —*Written by Matt Mauney and medically reviewed by Dr. Ashraf Ali, psychiatrist, in Precursors to Suicidality and Violence on Antidepressants: Systematic Review of Trials in Adult Healthy Volunteers. Journal of the Royal Society of Medicine 2016 volume 109 (10) Andreas O Bielefeldt, Pia B Danborg and Peter C Goetzsche*

"Trust me, I'm a doctor." *Really?*

Once back at her home again, I stall my mother by using delaying tactics as if I don't want to go inside. On the other hand, I hate being outside. It is difficult enough getting out of the car, but then I stop, standing in the driveway, shuffling my feet backward and forward. It is the epitome of my indecision—not knowing whether to go back or forwards. There is absolutely no rationality in this behaviour and I know it! Brief sparks of sensibility eventually drag me into the house and then, once inside, I become too stressed to go out into the sunshine again.

I spend approximately ten days at my mother's home with her and my sister trying to coax me out of my poisoned head and back into positivity. My nephews peer at me confused as to why their uncle just doesn't get over it and get on with life. To them, it looks so easy.

The weather has now turned to winter and with the cold and overcast conditions, the safety of a warm bed seems the best option. I am still avoiding any contact with people, which is part of the hyper-vigilance that has crept into my personality.

On the recommendation of friends and family, I am challenged with trying something new every day to start breaking out of the negative head-space I am in, but can't bring myself to do it.

"Are you coming with me to walk the dog, Craig?" Kim cheerfully urges.

Feeling quite positive that morning, I agree and start talking about how to move forward and how to do it quickly. The immediate solutions to my situation once again are clear, just as they had been in Riverside Clinic that first day of admission, and I know when and how to implement them. They have become quite clear and achievable!

Not fifteen minutes into the walk, and the cloud of emptiness and depression descend over me again! It is a tangible sensation; a cold washing over the body from head to toe. The medication from the previous evening has worn off and it was that which had been sustaining me and presenting the façade of clarity I had been experiencing! I believe this was inter-dose withdrawal.

> "Interdose withdrawal is where withdrawal symptoms emerge in between scheduled doses... It is a physiological need for the next dose before it is due."
>
> —w-bad.org

It is devastating! One cannot explain to another who has not been through this feeling of depression quite what it feels like. It is the worst insult to the human emotion and to humanity itself. If you have ever felt very down for a few hours, or even a moment, just try and imagine feeling like that for days, weeks, months, or even years as so many wounded souls still do.

These people walk our streets trying to look and feel happy. They are trying to appear like a 'normal, functioning person'. Stumbling down alleyways in search for the person they knew, the person that they used to be. Searching in bins and behind walls, up streets familiar to them and under bridges that shield them from punishing weather and critical eyes. They are trapped in this vortex by a mental condition, or because of being caught in a cycle of *Iatrogenic (doctor-prescribed) drug-dependence or protracted drug withdrawal* that may or may not be working for them. They suffer in silence, and they have my sympathy and understanding.

I was one of them, but I was one of the lucky ones.

PINE AVENUE

After the ten days were up, my sister and mother were tired of me staying at the house in Krugersdorp. I was draining their energy and affecting the lives of the older children there as well. The rotten tooth in the family mouth had to be extracted to still the pain for the rest of them in Krugersdorp.

There was another hole in my safety net. The small suitcase is once again stuffed untidily with my clothes and shoes that have followed me from Riverside Clinic, as I reluctantly and fearfully make my way to the car for the trip home. My children wait enthusiastically; Lisa has prepared a meal for us all. They have little idea of the depths to which I have deteriorated and are happy with my return.

With the early dinner complete, my mother and sister return home to Krugersdorp while I understandably stay behind with the children as this is where I belong. I have been given time off from work to recuperate and appreciate the opportunity to do so;

but nevertheless, I feel that I am shirking my duties and responsibilities and still have no vision ahead. Along with the medicated regime, the anxiety, depression, and exhaustion continue, unabated. The doorbell chimes regularly with uninvited guests and although I know they are being supportive, I fear their arrival.

These are loving friends and family. None of them are strangers, yet, I stare at the security camera screen whenever there is a possibility that someone might arrive. When and if they do arrive, I go into a panic. The anxiety extends to hyper-vigilance.

I am once again back in my marital bedroom after almost three weeks away from home.

My children have enthusiastically and generously rearranged the home for it to look welcoming and undisrupted. My bed has been moved around ninety degrees and placed against another wall near to the door. Some pictures have been moved to hang from different walls. It must be familiar for me, but different from before to create a new as is possible environment under the circumstances.

Since I had been away, my wife had removed certain furniture to adorn her new rented cottage. Things would have looked out of place upon my arrival and they don't want me to feel worse, so they moved lounge and dining-room furniture around tastefully, making me feel at home once again. It is a wonderful, loving, and caring gesture. I know I am loved, valued, and needed by them; yet it is increasingly difficult to reciprocate.

You were beautiful
To Me
I gave you my trust
You took it
Willingly
You basked in it and shared it
With us all
Love was unconditional then
And apparently forever
I have kept my covenant
But it matters no more
Shattered shapes that place
Emotions where we once were
Have now left only
Pillows dented
To be fluffed up by maids
Or family that care to notice
Perchance
To uplift
Our once proud and humble
Place

—*Craig Dawtrey*

My days are spent aimlessly watching time pass... literally. I clock-watch all day, achieving nothing until late at night when I retire to bed. Seconds and minutes are counted, for hours at a time; counting down the time to my next dose of medicine, and dreading the need for them.

Counting the minutes until the phone rings... Counting the minutes until a family member comes home... Counting the minutes until something changes for the positive— just counting.

My children respectively go to work and university each morning and I anxiously wait all day for them to arrive back home, intermittently watching the security cameras as they show me what is happening outside.

When they do return, I panic because once they step through the front door, they notice that nothing has changed for me and, by default, for them. I don't want them to see this, knowing it is destroying them; but once again, I have no way to solve it and move forward.

Everybody continues to urge me to "do one small new thing or activity per day" and this will start the momentum forward. Yet, I just can't bring myself to take that step... It is all too daunting.

The shadows of the cottage pane windows slowly and then quickly move laterally across the bedroom floor as the day moves on and away from me. They move from left to right, temporarily darkening the carpet. If I venture downstairs from my bedroom and into the lounge and dining-room area, I can observe the cottage pane clock in another place, bringing me the same bad news. And I just watch and think...watch and ruminate... Watch and fear... Watch...watch... clock-watch the sundial of sadness.

Each morning, I observe how habitual and territorial the local bird life is outside in my garden and develop a hatred towards a particular pigeon that mocks me at the same time each day. I can kill this airborne torturer... this defecator of walls.

Each morning, the same sound calls at my window. The same damn sound. Some of the other species of bird from my past sound happy, yet they cannot coax a smile from me anymore. I think... *the person I miss the most is myself. Where do I find the Craig I used to know?* The happy, smiling, friendly, sociable character that most people know. I can't remember how to laugh, how to cry, shout, express any emotion other than fear. And, fear of what?

I try to force myself to cry, wanting to feel tears run down my cheeks and feel something that remotely resembles human emotion! I force some sobbing sounds out from my throat that I recall as being similar to the sound of crying. I know I was capable of this in the past. This time, it is a feeble attempt and lasts for no more than a few seconds, but there are no accompanying tears or feeling. The performance is so bad that it should be funny. It should make me laugh at the image, but once again, no laugh is forthcoming.

Everyone is trying to get me out of this dark, sad place, but nothing works. The desperation in their eyes and actions are obvious, but are temporarily lost on me. I felt like a person in a television programme looking out of the screen and at the rest of the world—trapped in a small box on a stand, totally isolated from all people and everything meaningful and real. The viewers look on and occasionally encourage the picture; but the picture is not capable of directly and meaningfully communicating back.

This is called derealisation or depersonalisation and is described as follows; *"The primary symptom of depersonalisation disorder is a distorted perception of the body. The person might feel like he or she is a robot or in a dream. Some people might fear they are going crazy and might become depressed, anxious, or panicky.*

Depersonalisation may also occur because of extreme anxiety, panic, sleep deprivation, other mental disorders, and certain types of drug use or withdrawal. In some patients, for example, long-term use of benzodiazepines can induce chronic depersonalisation and perceptual disturbances."

> "Other symptoms may be feeling emotionally disconnected from people you care about, as if you were separated by a glass wall. Feelings of being alienated from or unfamiliar with your surroundings – for example like if you are living in a movie or a dream."
>
> —Mayoclinic.org

The problem I felt with persistence in this drug regime is that eventually I forgot what normality felt like and so had nothing to which to compare my progress or lack thereof.

"Am I feeling crap due to the medicine, or due to it not working?"

"Is it due to the side-effects of the medicine I am taking now, or are they withdrawal symptoms caused by the discontinuation of the previous attempted pill?"

"Do I ask for a bigger dose, or do I ask to have it reduced?"

At their insistence, I handed over my independence to the medical profession to the point that once I was in the system, it is very hard to see and fight my way out. I was to learn this later when things worsened.

Winter is now rushing past and I estimate the time of day by how the window pane lays its shadows down upon the floor and on the back of my curtains.

"Craig, why don't you put the heater on?" my mother enquires quizzically. My room has become freezing cold, but I don't allow myself to put heaters on as this will be spoiling myself, not believing I deserve the luxury of comfort. How I long for it, though. Although I know I haven't been the cause of the situation I find myself in, I am starting to blame myself for where my children find themselves. I am also a cause of their problem.

I start to regress in terms of everything human with any normal activity seeming odd and difficult, developing a need to be looked after, almost babied. I reduce my eating and drinking, figuring that if I do so, then I won't need to go to the toilet as that was what 'normal' people do!

I develop an irrational distaste and dislike for the feeling of water on my skin and stop shaving, with this culminating in me not wanting to wash or bath. Add to these a hyper-sensitivity towards light, sound, and smells, jumping at sudden noises, and squinting at any moderately bright light. All these stimuli become SO intense as to be offensive.

Armed with the knowledge that I need to eat something before taking the medicine, I irrationally decide that I don't want to eat and if I don't eat then I will not be able to take the poisonous medicine. All I do is delay the inevitable as eventually, I take the pills, but at inconsistent times, which just exacerbates the problem, continuing the bad habits I had started at my mother's home.

Over many days, I remain in my sweat suit and gown and squat in the passage to my room for hours on end with my head bowed down between my knees, trying to make sense of the situation and find a way forward. Bones peep through the sagging skin as my atrophied muscles fold tightly together and my body becomes a slovenly, squat ball.

The apparent contemplative pose is an image of a desperate individual trying to make sense of a cacophony of mental noise clogging a drained mind. The passage squat doesn't work as there is just too much emotional screaming to filter out.

Every day, my children return from university or work with a hopeful smile, only to find their father in the same miserable state they left him in. How earth-shatteringly sad I feel for them, but, alas, that is only in my mind as I offer no emotion at all.

I take no phone calls as I go into a panic the moment I see the screen light up with interest from another person. Making calls is also too traumatic. I stop reading e-mails and guess every day how many I am missing and panic about how it will be impossible for me to make them up again.100, 200, 300, 1000!

Human and technological communication is staunched... utterly. How will I ever catch this up when, and if, I ever return? This loss of business contact drags me further down as I start believing I have lost my job and poverty is waiting for me around the corner. Even when I am repeatedly reassured by my family that it isn't at risk, I struggle to see the positive and argue to the contrary—yet I have no proof of this.

The cell phone battery ultimately runs flat and I don't bother to recharge it. No battery means no calls, no emails, no communication, no stress, no logic. ALL is bad.

The glass is not half empty. There is absolutely no glass whatsoever!

Whilst I was staying at my mother's house our home had been sold, with my consent of course. I knew it had to be done but couldn't face it as it was a physical reminder that my happy family life had broken down irretrievably. Three people had three months to find a new home and I didn't even know who I was, never mind where I wanted to be. Lisa started to look for places to rent for a few months for us, as I was incapable and unwilling to do so myself.

I start to have a vision of the house now sold, everybody in the family moving out, and me sitting alone on the sidewalk of Pine Avenue—alone and broke. An old man with one suitcase, faded clothes to match his tattered memory, knees tucked into his chest, and head bowed between his knees.

Still catastrophising, I can't bring myself to look at or even discuss another home and use any stalling tactic to delay a discussion or viewing of properties. Lisa tries to get me to accompany her and I resist, knowing it must be done; but once again, I am not able to bring myself to do so. She bounds into my room ever hopeful after a day's hard work and attempts to encourage me to go and view a house. Knowing full well I must make this decision, I still avoid it unable to get myself into the car to go with her and Robert.

To compound issues, I have become agoraphobic and don't want to venture outside the house—not even into the garden. Everything is uncomfortable.

"Get into the car, dad. We need to go and view a house," urges Lisa as she tries to get me to view a property. Firstly, I am still dressed in the same clothes I have slept in and I can't envision myself looking at another living space. Her face crumples and her shoulders drop as she sobs at me, "Daddy, please! I don't want to be homeless!"

Neither do I, but I just stare at her, totally and absolutely devoid of any outward emotion. I feel sorry for her and myself, but can muster no empathy. Dead. Which I am, inside.

Lisa, with the encouragement of other friends and family, eventually manage to get me to go and look at two rental properties. The anxiety of merely climbing into the car is enough to make her tense.

The homes are tiny, cold, and such a step down from where we have come from that I will not see anything whatsoever positive in them. Even though the move is to be temporary, it feels permanent to me. The sight of these tiny homes reinforces the image of the steep slide in which I am finding myself. The one town-house is so small that I can touch the ceiling while standing flat-footed. Being in mid-winter doesn't help the cold feeling of the houses either.

I resist, and Lisa carries on searching without me. Once she has found a suitable home and I reluctantly agree it is good enough for our by-now-reduced-family of three, she tries to get me to sign the lease.

"Only for six months," I am told, but I just cannot see myself there or anywhere else. Stuck, just like I was told by my now-absent wife.

Have I internalized that comment to such an extent that my subconscious has adopted it as a delinquent and abused child and housed it within my soul forever?

By now, everything about me is stuck. One of the harshest comments uttered to me was becoming a reality. I guess when a man's ego has been so battered, it retains the bruise and stares at it to justify what has happened.

I stare at the pen for an hour whilst Lisa tries to get me to sign the document.

I just cannot bring myself to sign and have resigned myself to the fact that it cannot and will not happen. My life has been turned so upside down that I can't accept it. Any change is just too much more.

Lisa pleads and cries again, and I just stare, knowing full well what I am doing but still, I am not able or prepared to commit to the inevitable change. Still, there is no emotion on the outside and only sadness on the inside.

"Please, daddy. Please!"

I know I am losing my daughter and I can't do anything about it. The vision of being left on the side of the road with my family leaving, grows into visions of me on the street like a depressed, abandoned hobo.

Homeless. My family lost. No vision for the future. No hope. No money. Catastrophising, it feels far too real.

Winter was now in full swing, but nothing had changed for me. My winter had started during the previous summer when the darkness had enveloped me. I had progressively been lifted and then suspended in a black-hole. Weightless and with no sound. A cocoon of night. The winter of my discontent?

My mother has recently moved into the little cottage on my property to assist the children. In all truth, it is realistically purely because I cannot assist them myself. Every morning she gets up and I can hear her go into the kitchen to get the kettle going for some Milo or tea, bringing it up to me in bed. On cue, when I hear the door open, I freeze in anticipation.

"Morning, Craig. I have brought you something to drink." The bright voice attempts to lift me as she places the warm cup next to me.

"Thanks, mom, but I don't want anything," I lie, wanting the sustenance so badly. Refusing it for an hour or more, I ultimately take the tepid fluid down partially.

I don't deserve this, slips through my mind reflecting the state I have slipped into, completely missing the fact that my family don't 'need this' as well! Keeping myself just short of starvation, I later meekly spoon a bit of food down when it is too cold to enjoy.

Reading has become an activity of my past

altogether by now, and I don't want to spoil myself by watching television either. Reduced to the point where I stand at the back of the lounge whilst the rest of the family watch television I, like a deranged voyeur, peer occasionally around the corner to see what is being watched on the screen. Upon seeing Doctor Strange looking into the lounge the 'normal ones' encourage me to join them. Resisting like a scolded child or abused animal, I am afraid of the potential negative consequences, knowing full well there are in fact, none.

No matter what I coerce myself to watch, I have lost all forms of emotion and cannot laugh or smile, cry, or shout.

On the odd occasion I manage to make it past the doorway, I sit next to whichever child is on the couch, watch television, and don't say a word to them—not… one…word. Nothing. Knowing I wanted to, but I have forgotten how.

Tigger and Fable, the cats that have been with us for seven years, try to get onto my lap but to no avail. The cold shoulder I present to them is the polar opposite to the interaction that had seemed so normal a few short months ago. I can show no-one and nothing any affection whatsoever.

Shopping for groceries comes to an abrupt end, as this is now a challenge linked to the agoraphobia. As a result, my mother caters for each supper by going to the local store and buying enough food for four people for a day. I hear her return from the short journey up the road and hear the welcome sound of shopping bags as they follow her up the driveway and in through the back door that leads into the kitchen. I make no effort to help her with the shopping and pass on no money as support—being generous in sharing the nothing that I feel.

Occasionally, she escapes from Mr Desperado by retreating to her room in the cottage adjacent to the main house or going to visit my sisters, or her sister back in Krugersdorp. Thank goodness for family!

I don't want anyone to leave my home, but once they are away, I fear them returning. I fear them not returning. There is no malice from them, only fear from me. The days keep marching on, relentlessly.

Goose-stepping right at me...nudging me out of the way... Pushing me toward inevitability—toward the edge—needing to move physically and mentally, but no... Take the pills. The old man in the mirror with the wild, fearful eyes has a bearded chin that involuntarily twitches. His fingers shake continuously.

Mentioning this uncontrollable shaking to my psychiatrist during a later visit to her consulting rooms, it is explained to me as being as a result of my "deep-seated anxiety". Once again, with a stutter and anxiety-filled words, I explain that this had not been happening prior to me taking the medication. Deaf ears remain attached firmly to the sides of her head.

It is a dark, cold day when I stand up to move down to the kitchen. This day it feels different.

The front part of my lower leg muscle has lost all sensation. I can't raise my foot to clear the ground in normal perambulation and start walking with a 'dead' foot as if I am disabled. I have lost control of it and can't keep the front of my foot off the ground. It is as if I am paralysed in those muscles. Apparently, this is called 'drop-foot' and can be common with neurological damage or disruption. Whether this is physical or emotional, I am not sure, but the first appearance of the symptom coincided with the highly repetitive dose of Seroquel.

The Seroquel had been increased from only a single daily dose of 50mg at night to a new regime of 50mg in the morning, 50mg at lunchtime and if necessary, another 100mg at night. The Seroquel accompanied a double dose of Serlife (an SSRI) in the morning and Pur Bloka (a Beta blocker) with my breakfast cocktail. Then at night, Mirteron (a Mirtazapine, another tetracyclic anti-depressant) and the same as Remeron, previously prescribed by the original psychiatrist and Stilnox (a benzodiazepine for sleep) to round off another day of treading water!

How I hated this extreme regime. I delay taking the medicine until the blisters on my fingers burst from the activity of turning the pills over and over. Eventually, and in drugged contemplation—and just in case I change my mind once again—I reluctantly push them past my pursed lips and into my mouth, washing them down with water.

Every ounce of my being was constantly telling me something was wrong; how I hated this ruler of my mind! It was psychiatric advice dressed up in a psychiatric device.

Feeling this is far too much medication, I withhold

the Seroquel at night, rationing myself to the Mirteron at about 7:00. Settling in front of the television, I observe how my sight clears as the pupils shrink smaller and smaller, reflecting my body and mind's capitulation to the effects of the drug.

Outside the window and in the darkness of night, a halo appears around the lights. I do nothing and say nothing about its effect to anyone.

This is when I am temporarily the least stressed and along with this window of relief, occasionally join the family in some stilted conversation. Staying up late some evenings (three to four hours after taking the medicine), I know the medication is wearing off when my eyesight becomes blurry as the pupils dilate to normal range again. Dilated and deflated, I sink to the floor.

The quandary now is; do I take the Stilnox for sleeping in case it is too late at night? Staring at the pill for a few hours, I comically pop it in in the event it might help. Contrary to recommendation, I occasionally bite the Stilnox in half, in the hope that half-a-pill will be enough for the half-a-night I had left until daylight wakes the other people up.

The Stilnox works like a dream. It is only for a short period of time, as I am completely knocked out, but I always awake with a bump as the hypnotic effects wear off.

Oh, shit! I am still no further down the road towards healing and yet another day of hell awaits me.

On numerous occasions, I wait so long before taking the sleeping medication that I stay awake for the whole night. Wiping the sleep from their eyes, my mother and children drift into the lounge the next morning, hoping for my wellness. In preparation for their normal day, they only find me still sitting in front of the television.

"It's so heart-warming to see you up and dressed already, Craig," my mother says.

"I haven't been to bed yet," I respond embarrassed and fearful. This is soul-destroying for them, and I can see this in their sadness as they try to coax me to my bed at sunrise.

"Dad, you need to sleep," my children plaintively appeal to me.

"I know," is my muted retort.

And, I know, yet I still do not sleep and only make it to bed on the second day at 8-9 in the evening, a full forty hours after my last sleep. My family is worrying more and more as the day for moving home approaches, and I can still not and will not contemplate looking for an alternate living space.

The pending move is racing upon us and the household items need to be packed up for this eventuality. I am so deep down the hole that I can't see the light at the top. Where is the top, anyway?

Lisa, Robert, and my mother are all packing the clothes and furniture up, but I cannot and will not help. This is not an act of stubbornness, but a perpetual feeling of anxiety about the pending change. All I can see is the physical manifestation of my evaporating life slipping away. The cupboards empty out as the boxes fill up, trading places at emotion's expense.

Labels on cardboard jail-cells stamping a place in time on my recent past... lounge books, kitchen utensils, winter clothes, summer clothes, dining place-mats... her stuff, my stuff, their stuff—stuff it!

Finding a place half-way down the staircase, I sit and disbelievingly watch as this process continues in front of me. And it continues.... unabated. It must. I know this was inevitable, but I am not able to process the combination of events that has been thrust upon me and my children.

"I don't want to be committed to an institution," is my plea to the family; yet, I know that I look—and, for that matter, act—like I need one.

"We will never allow that to happen to you, Craig," is the convincing reply from my mother and sisters.

"I am so scared that if I am committed, I will never get out again as I won't have the heart left to fight." I am so tired and bereft of hope. Emotionally bankrupt.

As I sit on my bed one morning, the sun filters through the light curtains, "Craig, do you want to die?"

I answer meekly, "I don't know, mom."

"If you don't eat you are going to die," she continues.

"Well, at least I will die with my family around me," I sigh, unconvincingly.

At the time, I mean it, yet don't know if I fully understand the implications of what is said.

I do know this, though... Yes, it IS possible to die of a broken heart. I continue to shun food, and once supper has been made, I often hide in the bathroom with the door open, avoiding my family.

"What are you hiding from?"

"Nothing," a wheezy hiss escapes from my throat as I shuffle, embarrassed, down the cold passage.

I really want to be normal and be with them, but this is still oddly near impossible. Often, over a period of an hour or more, I scoop a spoon or two of cold food into my mouth whilst standing in the kitchen, never sitting down. I stare at them. I stare at the mirror. Trying to find my way out. And just NEVER see it.

The restraining wall is still right in front of my nose and it is, as always, impenetrable.

It is a dark and cool Saturday afternoon at about 2p.m. and the family, concerned, arrange to have a meeting. This will occur with or without me being present to discuss what should happen next. Just what I am afraid of might happen, my life has by now been taken over by others.

Lisa tries repeatedly that morning to get me to go to the car, giving me the option of accompanying her.

"If you don't come with, dad, then all the others are going to make a decision about your life without your consent or input." She makes absolute sense by saying this.

I stand rooted to the ground in my doorway as she cries in frustration. I won't change my clothing or shower. I am in dirty, overused clothes, and have not showered in days. I was a mess of matted grey hair and beard. "You smell bad and the others will notice."

I believe her, but have no emotional attachment to

the statement. It was logical... for others. Stalling for time, I take off my shirt. "Look how thin I am."

Why the hell did I do that? races through my mind as I watch her face crumple again.

> "Antidepressant treatment, not depression, leads to reductions in behavioural and neural responses to pain empathy."
>
> —Markus Rutgen; University of Vienna, Translational Psychiatry 9, Article number 164 (2019)

I am unintentionally breaking her down and once again, have shown no empathy for her. The medicine has killed all emotion.

She cries in frustrated terror at what has become of her beloved father. We have always been incredibly close as father and daughter. She has always been proud of me and I of her. Yet, here I am; her dad, emaciated and emotionally destroyed. Eventually, I decide to get in the car as the only amount of logic I have hooked into is that others will make a decision on my future and I will have no say in it if I do not go with.

The anxiety and agoraphobia have totally taken over my confidence, making the trip there agonisingly stressful and slow. The route to my sister's home has been travelled many times before, yet it feels horribly hostile and unfamiliar.

Arriving at Paige's home, it at least feels like neutral ground. Lisa and I cover the few steps from the car to the front door. As we walk into the home, everyone involved in the meeting is seated outside around a table. They greet me as if I am an unwelcome intruder; as if my being there will disrupt the decisions to be made about my own future.

They all sit; yet, I choose to stand with my back against a pillar as I look down the length of the table, subconsciously volunteering for the dunce corner. The weird, psychologically challenged family member that no-one wants to talk about, stands in front of the family panel. The atmosphere is cold and stiff, like a corpse of the fractured extended family awaiting an autopsy.

Clustered around the table, all sitting with perfect, tense, forced posture are Jackie, her brother Nicholas (also my employer), my sisters Paige and Kim, and lastly, my daughter Lisa. The family court has assembled to decide my fate.

They start with some formalities and then unceasingly stutter into a discussion about me and possible solutions. Well into the discussion, Lisa, in her desperation, mentions that I will not help with the packing away of the household items. Her comment has no malicious intent, but is rather matter-of-fact, illustrating where my faculties are at that point.

Nicholas suddenly blurts out at me, "You are a disgrace to your family!" As if this is a choice I have consciously made... He shakes with rage and clearly no understanding about my mental and emotional predicament.

Lisa leaps up from her seat. "Don't you fucking

talk to my father like that! You have no right to talk to anyone or judge them if you have not been through depression!"

My pride and joy! My girl. Myself. She has voiced what I cannot. My vocal and emotional surrogate. Yet, there still is no smile or outward emotion from me.

Lisa had—unbeknownst to us—suffered from depression a few years earlier and had managed to work through it with her psychologist, and as such identified with my situation.

Nicholas backs off and, still shaking with rage, dilutes his vitriol to, "You are acting disgracefully to your family."

This doesn't make me feel any better. In fact, it merely rubs salt into the gaping wound, reinforcing what I feel about myself, anyway. I look at the ground like a scolded puppy. Totally disempowered, they smear my nose in my own mess.

Further discussions are held about me until a direct question is posed, "Are you prepared to go to a recovery facility? You can't stay in the home and don't want to move elsewhere?"

Acknowledging the truth of the statement, I had made no progress, and was in fact, regressing.

Fully aware of this, I mumble a, "Yes, I guess so." I really don't want to, but am, like a school-child, hoping to defer the inevitable punishment by being vague and non-committal.

The meeting eventually ends.

Jackie and Nicholas depart, and the cold atmosphere instantly warms up the space they have vacated. The love and concern of my immediate family who had stayed behind, sweetens the bitter void for a while. Eventually, with no clear decision other than having to find a place for me to go to stay and find a solution, Lisa drives us home. I return to my cave upstairs to continue with my nothingness.

June passed into July, and then July raced by. Still, there was no change.

My late father's birthday came around. My mother, seated at the windowsill in front of me, looks across with tears in her eyes and says, "Wouldn't it be nice if there was a breakthrough today?" On dad's birthday," She continues.

Oh, yes, please, I think deep down. For everyone, for me. But still, nothing.

She starts to cry, and I stare at her, asking her not to do so, hoping that will help. Wishing that the shallow request will be followed with a good, logical reason I can still show no emotion. I hug her and still feel nothing.

"Don't cry, mom," I appeal to her unconvincingly whilst peering over her shoulder at the lawn outside the upstairs window. Dull. Emotionally dead. Stuck. Stuck. I hear the voice in my head echo. Stuck.

She hugs me in return and sobs, "I lost my husband and now I am losing my son." She gently wriggles out of my arms and hastens out of my room, trying not to look back. I stay in the room.

Purgatory sat somewhere between heaven and hell, according to religious doctrine. Yet, I had come to discover an unusual space. This was one where purgatory and hell were intertwined and suspended, swirling like a giant galaxy of confusion and self-doubt. All the planets revolving around the same central force; yet, every space occupied around it finding a different rhythm and time factor that would influence its relevance in that galaxy. As they traversed through space, the influence of the other celestial objects interacted with them and changed their points of reference. Every day the view would change, yet the planets had made no effort nor asked for the path that they were on.

Influence was ALWAYS from outside of their control.

PUSHED TOO FAR

"Enough is enough!"

The family had reached the end of their collective tether and insisted I go to a treatment facility. The decision was still partially up to me.

"You can decide where you want to go, but you have to go somewhere. If you can't make the decision for yourself, then we will do it for you."

I am terrified that if I go into any facility, I will be in it for life. In my mind, this is a REAL possibility. They have done their research and narrowed it down to a few options, but it is decided that Butterfly Lodge is the best fit. It is near to my home and I won't be far from the children. This, coupled with the fact that it offers alternative as well as allopathic treatments make it more suitable than other options.

It is a late Saturday morning when I am whisked off—OK, dragged out of the home to go for an interview to consider the facility's suitability. Butterfly Lodge is basically a domestic home in a residential area that has been converted to suit its purpose as a recovery facility. It feels better than any other clinic I had investigated and the smell of home-cooking adds to its appeal.

I still want to be at home with my children... my family. This option is however now impossible, as I am not capable of looking after myself, never mind my beautiful ones.

BUTTERFLY LODGE

After spending the full morning packing my bags, forcing me to shower (which felt like hell as I still hated the sensation of water on me), they try to get me to shave and eat.

They just simply want me to get the hell out of their hair. They are exhausted, and I understand, but just don't want to do any of it.

"I don't want to go."

"You have to go, Craig. You have no choice in the matter."

My sisters and mother try all morning to get me into the car for the short trip, but it is to no avail. They call Butterfly Lodge for some assistance from the qualified personnel there as my family are clearly not trained for this situation. When the owner of the facility hears we live less than one kilometre from Butterfly Lodge, she offers to come and try to coax me into the car. She stays for over two hours and talks politely initially, but she becomes progressively angrier with frustration at my intentional stalling. She has a facility to run and I am wasting her time, and am fully aware of it.

Whether I was under the impression that I could stall everything and everyone until I was miraculously healed, I am not sure. But I try. Sadly, I wasn't healed that day, so that clearly didn't work! The insanity of the moment!

The last solution proposed to my mother was for an ambulance to fetch me. That meant that I would summarily receive a tranquilliser injection and be sent under force, as it were, to Butterfly Lodge. This is the turning-point in my decision. I don't like the option of an injection or the trauma of my children seeing their dad forcibly being removed from home. My children love me dearly, and I them. I will NEVER do that to them, and so I eventually capitulate, climbing into my mother's car for the short journey.

As she slowly drives off, I keep the door slightly ajar whilst dragging my foot on the tar road, hoping to slow the transit to mini-hell. I will try anything to delay the inevitable. I was leaving my home I had lived in for seven years with my almost perfect happy family for the last time. I'm leaving behind a fractured and sad family and was now alone with one bag of clothes, just as I had feared might happen in that vision a few weeks prior.

The old male bull elephant kicked out of the herd. The tramp on the side of the road. They checked me into Butterfly Lodge on the first Monday afternoon of August 2016.

THE INNOCENT ONES

And along with his heart, she took his mind.
She took his soul, his spirit and his motivation.
She took his smile, she took his laugh.
She took his inspiration, she took his passion.
And although he has everything.
He is left with nothing.

Everything is nothing without soul, spirit, motivation.
Everything is empty without inspiration and passion.
Everything is lonely without a smile and the ability to laugh.

So together we will fill the mind.
We will ease the soul and find his spirit once more.
We will hold his hand and encourage the motivation.
We will smile for him, laugh for him.
And along with it will come the inspiration, the passion.
And from nothing, will be the birth of everything.

—Written by Lisa and sent to my family while I was at Butterfly Lodge

The drive to Butterfly Lodge is all of three minutes long. Being literally only two residential blocks away, I still feel I am leaving my life behind and moving into another world.

Upon arrival, I am over the edge with anxiety. The car door opens as I spill onto the floor near the entrance. Urging me toward the room I am to occupy,

I find myself standing in the doorway staring at the floor while the staff-in-attendance try to calm me down. They suggest I have *another* pill—Ativan, another benzodiazepine—to temper the anxiety. My mother and sisters are just outside the room, trying to look calm and disinterested in the medical melodrama playing out close by.

NOT ANOTHER PILL

This is the second benzodiazepine in the day, as the Stilnox is still prescribed to assist with my sleep. I don't like the statistics and quantities of benzodiazepine being thrown at me at all!

According to medical advice, this practice is risky when taken with another benzodiazepine as both are highly addictive drugs.

This is sacrilege to me, as I am already pumped full of medication and the thought of being enslaved to another one drilled into me is galling. Drugged logic still prevails in my mind.

"I don't want to..." I plead pathetically, turning the pills around in my fingers to stall; all the time asking ridiculous questions trying to distract the staff hence delaying the admission process even further. In their frustration the manager blurts out "If you don't take the oral medication, I will get an injection of Ativan and force you! The choice is yours, but it has to be one of the two offered!"

Fuck. Hobson's choice if ever there was. I opt to take the pills.

I am constantly being confronted by the two male attendants who look as though they are about to pounce on me if I try to escape. Looking through the eyes of a physically and mentally depleted body and vulnerable mind, they look bigger than I fear they actually are.

Feeling trapped like an animal which has lost its freedom, I analyse the situation, thinking, *I know I can take these two guys out; big guy first and then the small one.* In all this drugged confusion, I still manage to logicise that it won't be wise to take the fighting option, as then they REALLY will have a reason to strap me down and force me into a shitty institution.

Everyone there is trying to help me heal, yet, I have developed a 'me-against-them' attitude.

The struggle in my mind winds down slowly to a stop and with the others still around, I resignedly sit down on the side of the bed closest to the door. Taking the tiny pill, I slip the Ativan under my tongue as per instructions from the 'Butterfly Lodge Squad.'

My family sadly leave the facility with the parting promise, "We'll come and visit tomorrow, dad."

My power and independence continue to be eroded as I cede my life's control to others.

It is a frightening place to be! My scruffy room is cluttered with two single beds against a wall and a makeshift cupboard squeezed in at the opposing side. A rudimentary lamp perches atop a side-table.

There's an en-suite bathroom with a toilet, shower,

and bath through a door near my bed.

In the same way I have done for two months prior to this, I sit on the edge of the bed in my new, temporary home. Aunty Ativan starts to take her effect after a while and I resign myself to the fact that I need to eat, as it is supper time. With her chemicals she has re-arranged the chaotic, tortured thoughts into a neat row. At that point, I believe it is because I am healing; but in reality, it is the effects of her spell. Teasing me, she brings a smile to my face and a jaunt to my step and as I cross the twenty paces to the main house as the sun sets upon this first day. Stepping inside the main house, I confidently introduce myself to the other in-patients in the dining room and sit down to a good meal. Hell, I feel—and possibly even look—normal.

Supper is washed down with sweetened concentrated artificial fruit juice. Satiated, I walk back to my room, take a warm shower, and go to bed; just like normal people do. No strange sensation from the water this time.

That night, I sleep unusually well and awake timeously without the need for an alarm. I attend the group introduction and go for a walk with everyone chatting away happily. I feel good and am almost convinced the healing has begun. How could I be so wrong?

Halfway through the day, the cold sensation of depression washes over me again with my whole world dropping away once more as the bubble of happiness bursts... It was a drug-induced feeling of happiness I had been experiencing through that day, and the effects have unceremoniously worn off —not briefly, but instantaneously! Shockingly!

I had experienced inter-dose withdrawal once again. Anxiously, I ask if it is okay to have the Ativan again, but the request is declined with the reminder that it is "highly addictive". This is how one becomes caught up in a cycle of drug dependency.

Going without it then is the only option left and I attempt to make it through the day in mild withdrawal. Back into the hole I fall. Further. Deeper.

For the rest of the week the staff struggles to coax me out of bed, and even though they have a professional obligation and commitment to get me to eat, I readily miss meals.

The retreat from the world finds me reduced and limited initially to my home, then into a single room. It culminates in me being ensconced in my bed and finally, deep into my mind.

Into ever, smaller, spaces.

My regression is from adult to child, then to baby in-utero as I curl up in the foetal position with my head under the blanket where it is dark, warm, and safe, with no visible world to participate in. I find a place in the dark recess of my mind and slam the door, not knowing if I will be born and what the new world might hold for me.

After week one of settling in at Butterfly Lodge and being allowed some flexibility, one is expected —if not forced—to join in on activities. I hate them, not wanting to be involved in anything that feels coerced. Surely, I should want to participate? Ball sports? This feels juvenile, so I go to art class and do not draw anything at all.

They ask us to decorate a cover page for our file, and beginning the task, I defiantly scrawl my first name in rough pencil. Like a child... Intentionally... Stubbornly... Angrily.

Colour therapy takes place later in the day. I mumble to the facilitator that I don't want to participate in this either, choosing to watch the goings-on instead. Everything seems so childish and pointless, but the truth is that I actually can't start the task and neither do I want to.

Without the Ativan, the agoraphobia and anxiety continue to reappear. I don't go on another walk for days and confine myself to my room whenever I can. This is highly unproductive as I know, but that is nonetheless what I do.

On the second day, the social worker takes me for an interview to get a base reading of where I am for reference purposes. Appearing arrogant and disdainful, I don't like her at all from the moment I meet her. She glares in judgement at this adult man who appears so incapable and weak. Sitting on the couch opposite her, my anxiety and frustration levels are through the roof and show outwardly.

Why is she asking me ALL THESE QUESTIONS AGAIN!? I am sick and tired of repeating my answers and am so tempted to make up shit and see what might happen. Realising this will be a bad idea, I settle on complying for now.

Questions start from the breakdown of the marriage.

And my youth.

"Have you suffered from depression before?"

"No."

"Have you ever had a head injury?"

"Well I played rugby and did gymnastics for ten years, so probably had a few bumps, but does that count?"

"What was your youth like?"

"Good."

"Was there any abuse in the family?"

"No."

"Is there a history of mental illness in the family?"

Well, I think all humans are a little bit mad (but should I say it?)...

"No."

I start second-guessing my answers whilst simultaneously analysing what the counsellor is trying to draw out of me; all the while attempting to protect myself from looking mad enough to be institutionalised. This is still a very frightening possibility.

"What animals do you see on this picture?"

Fuck me, it's a dog, a lion and an elephant... Are you kidding me? flashes through my head, but thankfully, remains there, failing to pass through my clenched jaw. Prodding my inner brat, I am tempted in my mischievous way to say something like, *A goat, a devil and a bottle of whisky* to see what the reaction will be. Sensibly, I don't. Don't mess with the system and its priests. You might just be taken seriously and be crucified as an example to others.

"Mention as many words as you can in one minute, beginning with F."

Now, this is something I can work with! "Fat, final, fret, franchise, fur, French..." then I think fuck it! "Fart, flirt, fornicate, fuck..." I blurt out aloud!

It is clear where my anger is still targeted, and what is torturing my soul. The counsellor doesn't bat an eyelid as the minute flashes by. She doesn't seem to give a fuck!

According to the report from Butterfly Lodge, I was diagnosed with General Anxiety Disorder (GAD). I kept *"vacillating between blaming himself for making his symptoms worse by defaulting the medication, and blaming the medication for making his symptoms worse."*

> "General Anxiety Disorder is characterised by excessive, exaggerated anxiety and worry about everyday life events with no obvious reasons for worry...Daily life becomes a constant state of fear, worry and dread."
>
> *—WebMd.com*

On admission, the staff at Butterfly Lodge had been instructed to 'cold turkey' me off the medication I had been taking at home, namely the Serlife, Seroquel, and the Mirtazapine. I was only to be on my blood pressure pills and the Stilnox for sleep. I had made it clear that I wanted to be off all psychotropic medication, and my family had passed on the message to management.

I believe that the symptoms now being shown were the start of severe withdrawal from the discontinuation of the above-mentioned drugs. This can be so severe as to be termed "SSRI withdrawal syndrome."

> "It is common for dramatic side-effects to occur both during onset of SSRI medication as well as rapid cessation thereof. It can be so severe as to be described as a syndrome and can last from weeks to months with even years being claimed by some patients... and can, in part resemble the symptoms of anxiety and depression for which the medicine was given originally. However, the withdrawal syndrome can be distinguished from a relapse or recurrence of the underlying disorder by its quickness of onset (days rather than weeks). The withdrawal syndrome can be misdiagnosed as depressive recurrence, leading to prolonged treatment of patients who might not require it."
>
> —*DR. MA Horowitz PhD Prince of Wales Hospital, Sydney, Australia. 'Tapering of SSRI treatment an article in The Lancet Psychiatry'; March 2019*

Something that always intrigued me at all the facilities I spent four months recuperating in, was the large percentage of patients who smoked cigarettes. Admittedly, most of the patients that were there were being treated for addiction, and as we all know, nicotine is addictive. The addictions varied from alcohol to drugs and I even met a very unattractive, large young lady who proudly admitted she was being treated for sex addiction...

Huh? I thought upon the volunteering of this information.

"You have got to be joking!"

"Clearly, looks don't count."

The irony didn't escape me.

I then proceeded to worry about myself again.

——— ——— ———

Throughout the five months I was off work—including the three months at Butterfly Lodge—I did a lot of observing, alternating it with deep contemplation. The manager of the facility is a chain smoker and, sitting on the chair outside my room I discretely observe the way she smokes. Her quivering, stained fingers clench the filter tightly. Five long draws are always followed by long exhalations. Three deep drags in a row deplete the cigarette until only a third of it is left. Finally, a long puff out of her pert creased lips shroud her in a pungent grey aura. Completing the ritual, she stubs the cigarette out in an ashtray, filled to the brim with precisely the same length of cigarette butts.

Two miniature dogs the size of disabled cane rats follow her wherever her aura moves.

A bell has recently been commissioned, much like a school, to instil some form of routine in the patients. Just before the 7 a.m. morning bell rings for us to go to schedule, I hear her arrive with the two little Hitler-Youth Hounds goose-stepping ahead of her and yapping loudly.

You can always tell who is already awake by the doggy greetings… "Hello, Harry! Hello, Daisy!" This cheerful greeting is usually the sex addict, purring at the little stair-jumpers.

God, I hate those dogs so much. After a full day of yapping and in a moment of frustration, I hurl a boxing glove at Harry. The glove is as big as the hound, and the near-miss avoids helping him from the face of the Earth and into a new life with the lord dog himself.

Two years later and Harry had been moved to a new 'facility' or home, as he had bitten too many people. I cannot have been too wrong?

For the first few nights, I have the room to myself and am content with this arrangement, yet know I must eventually share with someone. There are two beds in the room and we are expecting a new patient from England.

Tom eventually arrives and introduces himself to the middle-aged whack-job sitting on one of the beds. My extended hand reluctantly shakes his after which I continue to be antisocial in every possible way.

During a regular schedule meeting and after only a few days of having been there, we are all informed that there is a new property that has been bought by Butterfly Lodge and we will be moving there in two weeks' time.

"Please, not another move!"

As crap as my room is and as basic as the facility is, I fear another change of environment.

Instability is traumatic, and I hate change as much

as I hate being stagnant, 'stuck' ... It rings in my head again.

Of all the possible ironies being added to my journey, the new property and home is in Pine avenue, only two residential blocks from my house and my children! My other terrible vision from months before has come true. I am on the pavement outside my home with one bag and the family gone, dragged further down the mine-shaft of fear and sadness.

How can I be in a recovery clinic away from my family whilst the children are on their own, merely two or three blocks down the road? Who is looking after them? What are they doing? Are they alright? What are they eating?

Shit, they are on their own and I am not there to help them! I can't help myself. I feel like more of a failure.

Much to our collective relief, the new Butterfly Lodge premises is much better than the previous one. It is lighter, bigger, better maintained, and has a relatively low wall where I can catch a glimpse of the normal life passing by every day.

I can see pedestrians, most of whom are vastly less financially privileged than I am. I catch myself wondering how they manage to look so happy when they have so little compared to my life, although at the time, I am an emotional pauper.

I used to drive my car down this very same road in my previous life. I wonder if I would ever be able to do that again. I strongly doubt it.

Standing and staring at the grass, the rockery, the

trees, everything in that small garden and patch of sky above it, I am continually looking for a way out of my mental situation. Looking for a sign, a pattern, a symbol, or a message in the grass, sand, or sky.

The gate that leads to the outside world opens, and for a moment, it taunts me into running out. Running away just two blocks down the road to the home and my children that are, for now, still there. The gate ushers the visiting cars into the parking area and then, once it is done with the teasing, it thunders closed—taking my world away from me again.

The gate teases me daily and each time I resist its temptation; settling for the world inside that I hate so much. The world inside the wall is designed to heal me, but, for now, keeps its secret potion to itself.

Still refusing to partake in any of the therapies, I show no interest in them, opting rather to sit and watch from within the group. Alternatively, I stand at the doorway, looking in.

I do not believe that I should be there, or that the stay is doing me any good at all.

I, as far as possible, also avoid any voluntary or compulsory sessions with the counsellors and therapists apart for the clinical one-on-ones with the designated psychologist and psychiatrist.

The sessions with the psychiatrist are the worst, as this was where I feel I am being coerced into taking the medication that makes me feel drugged and whacked out. By now, I have been off all medication for a number of weeks and all the previous medications have been withdrawn, cold-turkey. I am showing so many 'signs' of issues. I say 'signs' as I have no idea whether they are withdrawal symptoms from the discontinuation of medicines, or still side-effects of the drugs I had been on, still working their way out of my system.

In a subsequent evaluation with the director of the facility and the social worker, they come to the following conclusion about me:

~ He was unable to continue at Butterfly Lodge if he did not comply with the treatment protocol *(I had now also been prescribed Fluoxetine, which I refused to take)*.

~ He was unable to return home as his condition was so severe that the family were no longer able to support him.

~ He was no longer able to cope with the outside world.

~ He was no longer able to hold down a job, and unless he sought treatment, this option would be highly unlikely.

~ He was willing to accept that his condition left him debilitated.

~ He acceded that he would have to be independently assessed by a psychiatrist.

~ He would have to comply with medication prescribed and that he would in all probability be on them for life *(I always said to them I accepted this, but privately, would never accept it for myself. I knew anything to the contrary could spell disaster with consequences).*

~ He acknowledged his mental health at this juncture was critical and required immediate attention coupled with his treatment compliance.

Psychosocial concerns:

~ He blames himself for his current psychiatric breakdown, believing that his drug non-compliance has been a significant factor in his sudden decline in functioning *(at this stage, I was unaware of the probable withdrawal symptoms that were most likely the cause).*

~ His anxiety is evident in his restlessness, constant fidgeting, and inability to concentrate during sessions.

~ If he is asked a question, his anxiety seems to rise, he shows marked agitation, and struggles to respond, if at all.

~ He is overwhelmed by his inability to work and function adequately on a daily basis.

~ Craig is in crisis and is unable to function in the world at this juncture. His condition is critical and he needs to decide whether he is going to commit to therapy, the programme, and a pharmacological intervention, or not. Alternative care will be for him to go to Tara *(a large psychiatric hospital).*

And then one day later:

~ A psychiatrist came to see Craig and left him with a script for Fluoxetine and Craig is to continue with the Seroquel.

And the next day:

~ Craig in the office. Non-compliant with medication. No amount of coaxing and/or clarification could convince him to take the medication.

Their short-term plan was:

~ To have a joint interview with Craig, the director, and the social worker in this regard.
~ Failure to comply with medication should be a catalyst for an alternative treatment facility.

DEEP IN THE SYSTEM

The next day, two cars simultaneously pull into the parking area in front of the rooms as my children and estranged wife arrive for a family session with the staff at Butterfly Lodge.

What is this all about? I think as I peer out of the closed door in my room.

I so want to talk to the children and am within strolling distance from them when they leave. Once again, I fearfully resist the temptation and stay hidden out of sight in my room. Had I known what was being discussed, I would have collapsed from shock.

The day continues uneventfully until later when, following a group session that I am forced to attend, and stepping out into the afternoon sun, I feel my blood pressure rise. I shout out, "Surely, I know how I am feeling on the medication better that the psychiatrist does?"

This doesn't go down too well to say the least, as the manager blurts out in response, "You have been sectioned!"

My fuck, I think, "You can't do that," I wheeze back.

"Well, we have already," she says. And apparently, she can.

I am told that I am to be sent to Helen Joseph Hospital Psychiatric ward for observation for three days, and depending on the diagnosis, another three months at Tara Psychiatric Hospital might follow. If that does not work, then I could be sectioned for life!

I was to leave the next morning after my children and then still estranged wife had been to see me for a short visit. Once again, I do not sleep and instead haunt my roommates by spending the night sitting up in the chair in our room, contemplating what this means for me, my family, and my very existence. I feel traumatised by the inevitable knowledge that my children were coming to me tomorrow to say goodbye and none of us knows when this will stop, if ever.

The roommates would see the silhouette of me sitting in the room staring and not moving. *Do they feel threatened?* I wonder. I think I might have felt that way if the roles had been reversed. I am a dead man walking.

Along the path that swings and sways, her hips to the rhythm of my footsteps fall. Head bowed alone and lost. The way of the path that was formed by feet before mine. Cresting a gentle rise, I raise my head to glimpse an open patch.

Together, the family and friends that forged and filled my life are gathered. I hesitate briefly and then am willed toward them. Two hands part to break the circle and as I take the hands, the circle is once again complete.

The circle-of-support leans inward to view the hole in the ground. I tilt a wizened hand to see the branched veins that once were there have faded. They no longer look like my father's in life. The blue lines of life are replaced by patches of pink and a sallow yellow. Hands separate from the others track slowly toward my throat. A gentle touch increases in pressure as I press down, looking for a hint of life and a flow of life's blood. There is nothing. No regular throb. Their heads lift from the ground and stare at me...

Is it time?

The night passes slowly by and I once again avoid breakfast. The morning drags on as I clock-watch—terrified—and wait for the family to arrive. They eventually arrive and make their way to the office as I shrink even further into myself and melt into the tiny room.

I have nowhere to hide. If it were possible to find a space between the bricks on the wall and the paint covering it, I would have squeezed myself into it.

The meeting now finished, they come to visit me in the room along with the counsellor. It is the same social worker who I dislike so intensely, and she initially sits in on the meeting. She briefs them in front of me and tries to guide me through the meeting, all the while talking to me as if I am mentally disabled—the slow, purposeful drone of a teacher that has taught a lesson one too many times. Shortly and thankfully, she leaves and my children have some private time with me.

"He is functioning at the level of a five-year-old." is

her claim as she leaves the room.

Crying, my children plead for me to try and live—if not for myself, then for them. My son weeps and as he looks down and away from me, the teardrops splash onto the floor.

He can't bear to see his father in this state and predicament, and neither can I stand to see my son cry. Yet, still I cannot bring myself to hug them or say anything. My ability to talk still evades me as I stare on helplessly.

Their brief and emotional time with me now done, the children tearfully and reluctantly drag themselves out of the room and stand, waiting just outside the doorway.

It is then my wife's turn to come in and torture me further. I will never forget her statement that day—and more so, never forgive her for it. It shatters any remaining image I might have had that she has a warm heart. Following a character assassination of me and, "I can see you hiding in there," she finally hisses, "You are a parasite."

How could anyone who had spent a perceived happy thirty years together even contemplate saying THAT to one who was struggling with emotional and chemical torment beyond belief? More so, the torment had been instilled and voiced by the actions of the critic herself. She has made the judgement call that I am refusing to take the medication to stay ill, and thus institutionalised, and as such avoid any financial responsibilities. Why the hell would I want to do that?

I want to be free of my chains. I want to be in the

real world again and enjoy life and my children. I don't want them to be alone anymore! My children are still standing outside my door and they can obviously see the interaction.

As he glances through the open doorway, my son sees the look of hate on my wife's face as she glares at me. Through tears, he pleads to her, "Mom, please leave him alone."

She reluctantly does so and slithers out of the room, whispering vile incantations and spells; leaving me behind to deal with my tortured self. They all leave and the social worker comes back into the room; she suggests I have lunch before being taken to Helen Joseph Hospital.

"When did you last eat?" she asks.

"About a week ago!"

"When did you last drink something?"

"A few days ago," is my whispered answer.

She is shocked. Looking down at my hands, I observe how they look slightly different. My usually prominent veins have disappeared. They have, like my spirit, withdrawn deep inside my body. Low blood pressure has reduced their volume and changed the colour of my hands to a strangely pale pink.

"Why do my hands look like this?" I query innocently and ignorantly.

"Your organs are shutting down," she replies, nonchalantly.

Physical death is rushing upon me! "Shit, what have I done?" I think aloud.

Fearfully and hungrily, I wolf down the lunch

pizza, chasing it with a glass of sugary orange juice. Has this last-minute action stalled my perceived pending death?

HELEN JOSEPH HOSPITAL

"You have been sectioned and are going to Helen Joseph hospital for three days of observation, and then to Tara for three months!"

The horrifying words slip from the manager's mouth, cutting me in two and immediately escalating my rapid demise.

What the hell do I do now?

The simple answer was…nothing. With all my independence usurped and now firmly trapped in the psychiatric mental healthcare system, choices are no longer my own.

Terrified, deeper, and deeper I descend. My papier mâché life was being moistened and moulded into a picture I had neither any desire for or vision of. Hands clutching pens that ticked boxes on official documents were manipulating my present and future with scant regard for the outcome. It was a process and path that had no defined ending.

John, the driver, and Brighten (there is nothing bright about the man now), are the two orderlies tasked with transporting me to Helen Joseph Hospital on this dark day.

The others have gone, and Brighten stands in my

room and instructs me to move to the mini-van for the transit into Johannesburg.

"Can I pack a shaving kit?"

"There is no time. We will bring one later" he says sharply.

"Hmmm."

I hadn't been to the loo for days as I hadn't eaten or drank anything of any substance, and I guess the human pipeline just didn't have anything worth getting rid of.

"I just need to go to the toilet before we go." Hoping.

"Be quick, as it is late."

I am employing stalling tactics, and Brighten knows this. Searching so desperately for a good reason as to why I don't need to go to Helen Joseph. Spending ten minutes in the toilet doesn't assist me with coming up with one either. There is none.

Reluctantly, I eventually prise myself out of the bathroom and am whisked away onto the mini bus of terror for the transit to hell whilst the other patients look on with wide eyes. Knowing this isn't going to be a good experience, but climbing into the vehicle nonetheless, I ready myself for the trip.

Is this the beginning of my life's demise? How do I get out of this situation? I am not a criminal, but am being treated as one who has lost his independence as a convicted criminal does. Yet, no crime has been committed. How am I to reconcile this in my tortured mind? All the familiar landmarks pass by me as the minute's tick over towards who-knows-what.

Fuck! I am terrified. Truly terrified and yet, still no

emotion shows on my face. My biggest concern is that I didn't have my toothbrush with me; yet I haven't used one in days!

One of the biggest and most traumatic events in my life was happening to me at that moment, yet I was concerned with one of the smallest things possible—a bloody toothbrush! This was all I was capable of processing... Everything else was still too large to comprehend.

The apartheid struggle stalwart, Helen Joseph, had been immortalized by having a public hospital named after her. There was an element of irony once again ensconced in flattery, as the hospital had been previously known as the JG Strydom Hospital.

JG Strydom was one of the pillars of apartheid's creation and the National Party had named the hospital after him. It was a great medical facility pre-liberation, but had since deteriorated into a shadowy example of its former self, and I was destined for her. I would suggest that the renaming of a hospital, much as the renaming of a ship, is ill-advised, as it is rumoured to bring bad luck and, in this case, for me, it did.

John, the driver, and Brighten natter away, hardly noticing I am there, stuck in the second row of the mini-bus. It is a Thursday afternoon after all, and they want to get back to Butterfly Lodge as soon as possible to prepare for the weekend, and the dirty white boy in the back seats is hampering their plans.

We drive against the afternoon traffic to where the hospital is located on the outskirts of Johannesburg. As the vehicle slows down or stops at a traffic light, I once again have the urge to jump out, but where do I go to?

This time, it is not due to suicidal ideations, but rather the fight-or-flight mechanism seeking a way out of my predicament.

Neither fight nor flight are options anymore, as either one of them will result in me being in even bigger trouble than I already am. So, I must give the very little power I have left away, and swallow the minute amount of pride I have left.

The twenty-minute roller-coaster ride ends in the peri-urban area of Johannesburg and we slow down to a stop in the general parking. Throughout the drive, my sister, Paige has been trying to talk some sense into Brighten's head over the mobile phone.

"He's too vulnerable at the moment."

"He shouldn't be going there."

Brighten doesn't give a shit. This is not his monkey and not his circus.

I had been sectioned and he has a job to do, which is to get me to Helen Joseph and see me admitted. His body language transcends all verbal language and he is having nothing of her pleading.

I am escorted into 'admissions' and summarily given a file. "Why are you here?" asks one of the admission staff.

Had I had been a liar, I believe I could have convinced them I was an intern and had to check a few clients out. They would have possibly fallen for it and I could have confidently made my way outside and called my family to collect me. However, I have no confidence and no energy to think THAT deeply.

"I am here for observation."

The hospital admission room is a microcosmic representation of the demographics of the country where white South Africans make up a moderate ten percent of the population. I am the one percent representing my shade today, and stand out like a sore thumb.

By this time, the two apostles have bolted for the weekend hills.

The forms are filled out and I write under the 'Employment Status' section, 'Unemployed!'

I have never in my life before or since had to write those words down, and it rips my heart from my chest. The number of collective happenings that can drain one's self-esteem whilst in this mental space, is shattering.

'Unemployed' is not an accurate description of my status at this stage, as I am technically on sick-leave; but I see EVERYTHING in a negative and hopeless way.

A nurse ushers me to an admission interview with the psychiatry student who is obviously very smart; already a qualified doctor and well into the process of qualifying as a specialist doctor know-it-all. She has that look of disdain about her that accompanies academic arrogance. Tired and bored with the late Thursday afternoon duties, she takes a blood sample to give a reference base for future analysis of how the drug regime is treating me. They need to know if I am taking any other substances they are not aware of, and if my organs are showing any signs of distress.

As the needle is withdrawn, the cotton wool swab is given to me and I apply pressure to the small wound as per Doctor Know-it-all's instruction.

The medical staff had not taken into account my lack of interest in anything. I haven't pressed the swab down hard enough or long enough, and as I sit, I watch as the blood trickles down my arm and stains the long-sleeved shirt I am wearing. The red blood stains the blue shirt black and the warm fluid cools and crusts as the cold and uncaring hospital drags me into her clutch.

It doesn't matter, as crusted, cold, bloody, and dirty unkempt clothes are appropriate camouflage in this place. This shirt and the pants that hang loosely from my emaciated body are the only pieces of clothing I have there with me. The belt that shows evidence of an additional recent piercing, tries desperately to keep the baggy denim jeans from losing its battle with gravity, as I struggle against looking too much like a tramp. Both the denim jeans and the tattered mind are failing horribly.

Awaiting the interview by Dr Know-it-all, I sit on a typical government bench in the hallway and watch the rest of Thursday's African chaos pass by. An emaciated man that is obviously an addict sits on a gurney opposite me with his long, greasy grey hair and skinny, dirty, stoned body. He is strapped down whilst he dazedly attempts to wring his scrawny arms out of the straps restraining him. His glazed, staring eyes track upwards slowly and then down again as his hands and grubby fingers scratch and claw at the restraints around his wrists. His drugged mind appears to give him no clue to the way out of the straps and his mental predicament. I briefly glimpse the terrifying possibility of finding myself there in that place, in the future, in that body, on that gurney... like him!

From around the corner comes the screaming of a man seemingly possessed. It is followed seconds later by a tortured mind ensconced in a young black man's body on a wheelchair being propelled by another clearly frustrated hospital orderly. The possessed man shouts and barks out incantations, prompted by toxic responses to his drug overdose whilst his friends and his white older boyfriend watch coyly from the opposite wall. They knew the possibilities of drugs, yet seem embarrassed at the unexpected outcome of overdose!

He curses the people in Sandton and other faceless targets by name. He growls and howls whilst the visions in his head toy with his intoxicated mind. Those people are going to die, and he is going to make sure it happens.

Restrained and injected with a tranquilliser, he starts to calm down, much to my relief.

My normality is disrupted in any case and the additional chaos adds to the distress.

After a short while, Doctor Know-it-all returns and completes an admission interview with me, writing down her evaluation.

The admission medical report states:

Main diagnosis:

- General Anxiety Disorder;
- Adjustment Disorder;
- Major Depressive Disorder;
- Mental state examination;
- Well-groomed (the comparisons at the hospital were clearly very low);
- Unable to keep still (I believe this could have been Akathisia, a potential side-effect of psychiatric drugs or withdrawal symptoms);

> "A movement disorder characterised by a feeling of inner restlessness and inability to stay still. People may rock back-and-forth, fidget or pace. Complications include suicide. Causes are antipsychotics, SSRIs, untreated schizophrenia, Parkinson's Disease metoclopramide and Reserpine."
> —Wikipedia

- Fiddles with beard, hands;
- Mood low;
- Restricted speech;
- Delusions;

- Plot objectively hallucinating?
- Poor insight;
- Rubbing his nose and ears until red;
- Very guarded;
- Apsychotic;
- No insight.

She then prescribes:

- Fluoxetine 20mg;
- Seroquel 200mg;
- Propranolol 20mg.

"Is it necessary to give me such a high dose?" I curiously and fearfully ask of her about the Seroquel.

Her response is a glib, "I prescribe up to 600mg to some of my clients!"

So here we go again! Back into the medicated regime, I think... From the fat and straight into the fire!

> "Kindling is described as a neurological condition resulting from repeated withdrawal episodes. The central nervous system becomes hyper-sensitised and hyper-excitable—each subsequent withdrawal leads to more severe withdrawal symptoms than the previous."
>
> —*Wikipedia*

I had been 'Kindling' and now was reinstated into the cycle!!

The admission, blood tests, and interview now complete, my Thursday night experience slips down to a lower and lower level as the nurse escorts me to the psychiatric ward. She doesn't talk as the echoing footsteps lead me through abandoned wards and up elevators that clunk and shake dangerously. Helen Joseph is shaking her head in disgust. She is not welcoming me in at all and is not happy to have me as her guest.

A security guard is placed on the other side of the security gate of the psychiatric ward; the gate that separates the free people from the incarcerated ones, and the sane from the insane. The guard opens for us, and the orderly leads me across the threshold and into an unknown world—a place behind bars; a place of physical and mental incarceration.

The metal jail doors slam shut unceremoniously and unforgivingly behind me. Taking a deep breath, I take another step down a rung of the emotional and self-esteem ladder, fearfully wrestling with the dual challenge of finding a way out of my mental anguish as well as the physical incarceration that I now find myself in. It is a swirling, misty haze of disturbance and disruption.

During my national service as a nineteen-year-old conscripted soldier, I had to stand guard duty at 1 Military hospital in the city of Pretoria. Part of the beat took place in a deserted section of the massive hospital, which was hauntingly intimidating at the time. Walking into the ward brings flashbacks of that time and place, but now it is much worse, as I have no control over it.

Back then the guard-duty beat would have alternated between two hours on and two hours off, with the cycle repeated over a twelve-hour period. There, in that era, I would have seen an end to the guard duty, eventually. Yet now, here I was to be in Helen Joseph Hospital for five days of analysis and observation, and depending on the report, I could be sent to Tara for three months. If the three months at Tara did not yield a positive result, I could be sectioned for life with the control of it handed over to the psychiatric 'professionals'!

It is a dark day of fear. Am I in for life?

Having a guard in attendance at the entrance to the psychiatric ward seemed a bit extreme, but it was necessary, as I was about to find out. Soon after being admitted, and once all the relevant boxes were ticked and scribbled on admission papers, I am handed a state-issued sweat suit.

"Put this on," mumbles the nurse.

It is a dark blue colour and has a badge embroidered on the left chest side, marking us as patients of Helen Joseph psychiatric ward. Being branded as a psychiatric patient is not my proudest moment, albeit temporarily.

I am summarily relieved of the only civilian clothes I have with me—a pair of jeans and my blood-stained shirt, which are packed into a transparent plastic bag and placed in the store-room in which I have to change. They now accompany the other patients' bags-of-hope until who-knows-when…

"Will I ever be well enough to get them handed back to me?"

The only visible remnants of my normal life are crumpled away along with my hope in a bag and stashed in an arbitrary state-owned store-room. They allow me to keep my semi-formal black, polished shoes and socks which emphasise my image of a mental patient. They were certainly NOT designed for wear with a sweat suit.

If anything, the sweat suit is fleecy-lined, and thus relatively warm for the unheated space in which we are incarcerated.

"Follow me," the nurse ushers me on a few paces from the store-room and on to the nurse's station. The nurses on duty hand me the drugs I had been prescribed, including the anti-psychotic drug, Seroquel, which I am instructed to take right away. There is no place for an argument here and, naturally, nowhere to run. So, once again, I submit to the deep trap of the mental health-care system with no idea how long I will be there or when I might get out.

I share the dormitory with another ten wild men where the lights never seem to go off!

Add to that the ten more patients packed into an adjoining room through the open door behind my bed. All-in-all, twenty psychiatrically challenged individuals shared one room with a view of the real world that I know but cannot reach through a window only five meters away.

Further down the passage, five other patients are accommodated in a high-security room that is in fact a cell, and is locked at night. Is it for their safety or our safety? I am not sure.

The panorama out the window is familiar, but I had only seen it from much better vantage points in Johannesburg and in vastly better times. There are no curtains, no heaters, and no soul to this ward, yet it seems to suit me as I become one of the living dead. It is a life ruled by medical staff, drugs, clocks, and shadows.

Within a few minutes, the Seroquel takes hold as a drowsy calmness settles over me. The nurse guides me to a shower and generously supplies me with a piece of cloth to dry myself.

I am not aware of any other patients around, as my extremely drugged shower takes place in a small communal bathroom—a bathroom so much worse than the army barracks I had experienced many years prior. The walls and floor are stained with years of badly aimed urine and institutionalised neglect that accompany a lack of cleaning and caring. A patchwork of vinyl tiles is missing and the scars of the torn floor expose the grey cement base of the bathroom. An aroma of drug-infused stale piss drifts across the narrow corridor and burns my over-sensitive nostrils.

The Seroquel dose must have saved me from the awareness of time as I completed the 'shower', dried myself, and must have gone to sleep as at this point everything was a haze.

A tired, drugged eye slowly wakes up to a vision of Jackie standing in the doorway of the ward. She is in her gym clothes and I wonder, *why is she here so late at night?*

"These drugs they gave me are making me so drowsy," I slur at her framed image.

My soon-to-be ex-wife passes on the partial diagnosis, told to her by the doctor who admitted me, "You are delusional."

A later look at Google Dictionary, tells me that being delusional is described as holding idiosyncratic beliefs or impressions that are contradicted by reality or rational argument, typically as a symptom of a mental disorder.

My opinion of course to her is that I am fine and don't need to be there; "The drugs make me APPEAR delusional." Her smirk accompanies the deaf ears once again.

The drugs take hold again as I drift off back to sleep.

The next morning and with the medication having mostly worn off, I dazedly shuffle to the bathrooms only—and shockingly—to realise that there is, in fact, no shower in the unit and that it was a pure figment of my drug-induced mind! Am I going mad or is it the drugs? I am starting to doubt myself! I had 'showered' by curling up under the tap in the bath.

Jackie had, in fact, not been there the previous evening either. Instead, she had visited early that morning, and that is why she was in her gym clothes! I was still stoned by the 'medicine' I had been prescribed and had lost track of time!

I am terrified of what is happening to me. Personally, I think it suited the agenda of all those concerned, as it reinforced their perception that I was loopy and 'sick'.

My state-appointed sweats are starting to feel comfortable. It is ugly, but I let the fashion-conscious moment pass and settle for its practicality as it is warm at least. The drugs once again put me into temporary comfort as I sleep deeply. For a while.

"Bath time, bath time!" rings out through the doorway.

You have got to be joking? It is 4 a.m. and, as hospital staff, they wake the patients up for a bath. Twenty psychiatrically challenged males are jolted from slumber to clean themselves in a Hobson's choice of two filthy baths. Joining the queue is not a part of my plans. To join is to conform, and to conform will be an acceptance of my mental 'illness'.

I refuse to bath for five days, as the then acceptable drug-induced 'shower' had been replaced by the bath and I was NOT going to sit or stand in THAT bowl of filth again!

In the same ablution block, there are two toilets for the men to use. One of them isn't working at all, yet that minor issue doesn't put some of the patients off. All the images one might dredge up linked to a toilet that doesn't work in a psychiatric ward are there for all to see in the bowl. Floaters and sinkers and dark urine and seats sprayed as if everyone has been trying to mark their territory.

I, for one, don't want to see it! This is definitely NOT my territory! The other one is so filthy that I refuse to use any toilet for five days! Yes, it can be done.

Lying on the bed, my head under the duvet, hiding from the reality facing me from across the passage. Shrouded by bleached sheets and white pillows, I am a nightmare in white satin, if ever there was!

I quickly discover that there are a few kleptomaniacs incarcerated with me, and as a result, everything of value has to be protected. That most certainly includes the state-issued bed-linen. There is no place to safely lock them away, and the small cabinets next to each bed are broken anyway.

I choose to either sleep with my shoes on my feet, or under my pillow. It doesn't matter to me if the old black polish rubs off on the sheets overnight, as at least the shoes are still there the next morning. It is amazing how, when the mind goes from riches to rags, one will defend with one's life objects that seemed so menial and minimal in the past. It was so different in the times of emotional and physical wealth.

During the first night, I awake to the tugging from a deranged young black man who is trying to pinch my shoes from under my pillow. My hands clutch them loosely, and I tug them back angrily from his dirty, corrupt hands. How low could I go? Further, apparently.

The same fruitcake that tried to steal my shoes would spend his whole day—and, if awake, his night—trying to steal anyone's and everyone's items. On the occasions he managed to succeed, he would then contentedly wear them, defiantly parading around with them until Fruitcake number two would liberate them from him once again. This process would continue until the goods found their way back to the original owner. This asset liberation was rather violent on occasion.

One day, after the liberation of someone else's asset-of-little-value-that-means-a-lot, a few of the other patients—with a distinct lack of self-control—decide to take revenge on Klepto-Number-One. They huddle as they not-so-surreptitiously discuss the mission and then set out with the organised chaos one would expect from a psychiatric unit, to get the asset-of-little-value-that-means-a-lot back for the original owner.

The 'Psychiatric Asset Recovery Unit' track Klepto-Number-One down, grab him, hold him down in front of me, and remove the stolen goods whilst another asset-of-little-value liberator summarily kicks him in the head for good measure. The shoes were now recovered, it was mission accomplished.

Naturally, I sit and watch, transfixed, drugged; making sure not to catch the eye of some other 'psycho' or show empathy, in case I am seen as a sympathiser.

The nurses on duty do nothing to stop this and won't get involved in any way. They don't seem to care at all. They are merely there to complete their shift and, once replaced by the new shift, the preservation of the status quo of mediocrity and under-service is maintained. There is no place for the Hippocratic Oath in this place for these 'nurses', and certainly, no appropriate bedside manner is offered as required and expected from their profession. Florence Nightingale would have been shocked and likely have fired the lot if she had been alive and in charge.

Meal times with Klepto bring on a new concept in fine dining. There is a communal mess hall into which all twenty men are ushered. To the left of the entrance is a basin which is there, naturally, for hygiene purposes.

Four long wooden tables are squeezed into the room with between four and ten chairs scattered around each table.

Each patient stands in the queue and, in turn, receives their daily bread. Taking the plates and the plastic knife and fork, we walk into the dining room and move to find a seat around a table. My objective is to try and avoid Klepto-Number-One and any other seemingly dangerous patient, keep my eyes down, finish the food, and then leave the area.

Halfway through one of the lunches, I happen to look across at the basin. There, to my disdain, is Klepto-Number-One washing his hands in his own urine! He often paraded around in the nude. Now, he has unceremoniously slapped out his pelvic trunk and is bathing his hands in his own wee in the basin in the dining room!

We find this rather odd, but nobody comments. It is too dangerous, so we just look back down at our plates and try to finish what is there. Would the chief urinator from the dining room qualify as a 'piss-cat'? For five days after this incident, the basin remained unused.

Starved of calories, I discover a taste for a South African staple: mealie-meal with lots of sugar. It is often given to us for breakfast. This is the most basic of African meals and is made from ground corn (or mealies). I would normally balk at the pale porridge on the equally pale bowl, yet every morning, I manage to finish eating my portion. I have lost all my control, yet in my state of self-deprivation, I am controlling something, albeit negative.

There is never enough food for second helpings.

It is state catering on a state-funded budget. When you are reduced to a less-than-insignificant individual, you tend to evaluate and assess everything from the changed base. Bad food tastes fine, and moderate food tastes awesome!

The female patients join us at mealtimes; the rest of the day, they are separated from the men for their own safety. There are only about five women housed in a separate room down the passage and on the other side of the dining room and nurse's station.

During one of the mealtimes, I notice a lady that looks as scared and alert as I am. Having no idea what she is in there for, I briefly glance across the table into her eyes that look familiarly fearful. We have a brief, cursory discussion.

"Why are you here?" I query.

"Severe anxiety and depression," is the response. "And you?"

"The same. I have been sectioned, but I really don't want to be here. I am supposed to only be here for observation."

"I also hate this and want to get out," she agrees.

We have decided that neither of us should be here, but how does one break out from this physical and emotional space if control of one's life has been handed over to others?

I think about all the other patients who suffer from illnesses that manifest physically rather than mentally; they still have some semblance of control over their lives and choices.

Somehow, the psychiatric patients are led—and, dare I say, controlled—beyond by what is perceived as reasonable treatment. Yes, many need to be looked after, but the vast majority hand their lives over to medical arrogance and chemical dependency. They live fear beyond fear; alone, even if only in their minds.

Once the support of family is gone, one is left alone to struggle with the microcosmic chaotic world in which you are left behind, both within one's head and in one's surroundings. It's a bit like life, but without the champagne and roses.

By the morning of day two, I have started to identify the various personalities and thus, my potential threats. Sleeping in the bed across from me is a particularly disturbed black man in his mid-to-late thirties. He loudly babbles on all day in two-hour shifts. Thankfully, he alternates this behaviour by sleeping off his dementia for another two hours before waking up abruptly to repeat this routine. This carries on all day and all night.

The problem with the behaviour is that he is highly aggressive and doesn't talk nicely to the 'old man' sleeping opposite him. "Old man, look at me," he snaps with wild eyes.

There is no response from me, although I am insulted with the 'old man' chirp. "Old man, talk to me. I am clever!"

His maniacal eyes change as he slips his focus to a poster on the wall where a 'patient's bill of rights' is pasted. He frantically reads it in an attempt to explain the rules, trying to convince me of his sanity. A brief glance at the violent, crazy eyes convince me he SHOULD stay firmly in this place and that I will stay silent and not talk to anyone here—ever.

In a moment of temporary silence, Klepto-Number-One snatches the duvet off the Violent One's bed (whilst I am still under mine), proceeds to baptize it will all the snot he can muster, and throws it onto my bed in order to set me up. I grab it and throw the duvet back onto the other patient's bed to get both the snot and duvet off me, whilst transferring the blame right back. Bile rises in my throat as I choke back unwanted vomit. As a self-confessed snotaphobe, this tests my tolerance to the core!

I am being framed... Bed-framed! Being implicated in anything untoward amongst twenty mentally ill people where there is no logic and contradictingly, 'sanity does NOT prevail', is ill-advised.

Evading the pending confrontation, I step into the passage only to see one of the ladies walking toward me draped only in her hospital-appointed sheet. She has managed to create a crude example of her rural clothing that possibly makes her feel at home as she proudly stomps up and down all the time in conversation with her 'passengers'. Is it perhaps a link back to her family roots and what reminded her of home? She parades like this every day and night, including meal times. Ironically, some of the male patients are disgusted by her perceived lack of feminine humility, forgetting we ALL look tattered.

"Meds time! Meds time!" The words echo down the corridor and into the wards.

Not here, too?

It is eight o'clock in the evening, and time for the twice-a-day drug parade again. I am so tired of this call to arms by now. Every psychiatric institution seems to use the same call to medicate and I must conform; otherwise, Tara Mental Hospital is my next destination. Why is this call so sugar-coated as to be referred to as 'meds'? Is it to convince us that the chemicals are not doing any harm? Why not be honest and say; "it is time to take your drugs?"

The lost boys stand in a queue to receive their unholy communion of poison. The room keeps me safe and away from the hated queues until the nurses fetch me. I am still reluctant to take the medicine as I can feel its negative effect daily.

After many hours of resistance, I must comply and take the medicine as I am last in line and the only one stubborn enough to persist. Additionally, I don't want to run the risk of totally disobeying orders and being incarcerated for longer than initially prescribed.

I shuffle and limp on the one 'dead' foot back to the room. There, I sit on the bed and once again avoid contact with all and sundry. I offer no conversation and no eye contact. These are NOT my friends and there are none that I feel will ever deliver a protracted relationship. I will not be associated with them as I am NOT like them, and I will NOT be here for long—I hope.

A voice soars from down the hall! An untrained baritone blurts confidently as it starts doing its voice exercises for its pending operatic performance. Every day, a sixty-year-old man with an untrimmed beard, would sit on the smoking room and warm his voice up before bursting into a vague, loud, and aurally toxic rendition of 'Paint Your Wagon'. He was shite and he reeked of stale cigarette smoke.

He would proudly tell the nurses that he was the beneficiary of a trust fund and was, in fact, wealthy. From the reactions that I observed, the nurses were unconvinced. In reality and in retrospect to the outside, un-medicated observer, this could have been seen as funny, but I didn't see it that way.

A Nigerian drug dealer is admitted on Saturday evening after sampling a bit too much of his wares. His large body and drugged mind barge its way through the unit. Once inside, he promptly proceeds to break off bits of the wall in the passage until he is restrained by security. Amid much shouting and warning, the largest security guard wrestles him to the ground, cuffs him, and whisks him off to jail. He returns the next day a much more subdued puppy after being criminally charged and having sobered up.

The cosmopolitan chaos of Helen Joseph's

psychiatric ward was spearheaded by an elderly Indian man who would spit curse-words and vomit vitriol from the moment he awoke until he retired from the clarity of daylight. He only had a few rotten teeth left between the spaces vacated by those that were long gone. He seemed to gain strength from the chaos caused by the other patients that ensued at erratic intervals throughout the day. Crowd violence seemed to be his trigger.

It is day three of my daily regime of avoiding communication with everyone there. As I lay quietly under the duvet, my fellow Indian patient decides in his perceived power pose to pull the duvet off my bed. Attempting to evade the flying snot and spit he spewed, I shoot up, instinctively protecting one of the few assets I have at that stage, ripping it back aggressively.

It is difficult to see yourself as powerful and assertive when the mind and confidence has been drained from you, but it is a big step in spontaneity and fight back from my side. My puny body—that by now weighs less than 70 kilograms—doesn't help in this regard, either.

He seems to see the anger in my eyes, which is a nice change from the sad, scared look I have portrayed for so long. Backing off briefly, he nervously assesses the spontaneous event, all the time dripping saliva through the spaces between the last survivors of the dental holocaust in his mouth. He aborts his plan. He was lost forever in a maniacal maelstrom.

This apparition would also drool and drop food down his chin when eating anything in the dining room; this severely tested my vomitometer. Ah, another mind to avoid, I noted.

Evening three of my 'observation' and I am introduced to a master class of drug abuse observation. I sit on the floor at the nurse's station where I sometimes feel safe in the front of their uncaring eyes. I occasionally hang out there so that if anything untoward happens, they will have been there to see it.

This evening, the pretty black boy (who had wanted to kill everyone in Sandton on his admission), sits on the floor, too. He introduces himself to another patient. He tries in vain to introduce himself to me, but I continue to avoid any conversation.

I don't want to become familiar with that place or anyone in it. Civility has some place here still but I will not be dragged in. They chat without me, yet loud enough for me to hear, as they have nothing to hide.

Glancing across to my right side where they are, I notice him opening a little square stamp before summarily licking it. It is not much out of the ordinary, I think as he passes on a similar stamp to the man next to him.

The nurses keep chatting. They take no notice of what is happening right under their noses. It is either that, or they genuinely do not give a hoot. Eventually, at eight o'clock, they dispense the prescribed medicines and our so-called bedtime nudges its way in. I retire to my cot near the door.

The lights go off. The lights go on. The lights go off again.

The white duvet covers my head as I search for

slumber. It should be relatively easy as I am still on 200mg of Seroquel, so sleep is temporarily chemically enforced. A few moments of peace is abruptly broken by an explosion of chaos! The light is back on and everything is loud, bright, chaotic! Drugged youth. In the psychiatric ward. In front of the nurses.

Loud chaos ensues.

There is shouting and arguing and music and smoking in the ward!

Patients move constantly in and out of the doorway and the passage and the rooms!

I am so unbelievably tired due to the lack of sleep and the drowsiness caused by the medication, but keep my head under the duvet where I can't be seen and cannot see, hoping the chaos will stop. I have mastered the art of shutting out noise by now, but THIS is nigh impossible!

The chaos carries on all night long. The nurses eventually lift their fat, lazy arses off their seats at the nurse's station and intervene, but the effects of the drugs have worn off and it is already 'bath time' again!

Already!?

Fuck, please... No!

4 a.m.

I stay in bed; I refuse to get up and refuse to go for the medicine and delayed breakfast until the last minute when one of the patients comes to fetch me, forcing me to the station at the behest of the nurses.

I must eat. Every day is the same process... The same goddamn routine!

I was supposed to be at Helen Joseph for three days

of observation. As luck would have it, I was admitted on a Thursday and as such was 'cursed' by a weekend in between, so had to stay for five days instead!

We usually have a brief appointment with the allocated psychiatrist each day; yet, due to my Thursday admission, the psychiatrists cannot see me until after the weekend. As much as I despise their involvement in my life due to the situation I find myself in, I see them as a bit of a safety net. I was destined to enjoy forty-eight hours with the wild bunch trapped in psychiatric hell!

There is a tuck shop in the unit. It opens at various times over the five days I spend there. Not remembering when these times are, I do not pay any attention to it as that will entail spending money and I have none. I have abdicated any emotional or physical wealth and any indulgent spoils will be just that—spoils; and that is for 'normal' people.

The odd (and I say that loosely) person offers me some of the tastes of heaven from the tuck shop and as much as I would love to say yes, I abstain. I do not want to accept anything from anyone, because if I do, I will potentially owe a debt that could place me in an awkward predicament out of which I might not be able to get too easily. I prefer to continue isolating myself with no connection to anyone or anything.

Being fully aware of Klepto-Number-One by now, I wear my wrist-watch constantly; I always have as without it, my wrist feels undressed. Ironically, the watch battery had run flat a few weeks prior to this, but I neither want to take it off or have the battery replaced in order to get it working again. There is some tenuous emotional link between the watch on my wrist and the security of the life that I have left behind, and it helps me feel just a little bit safer.

The wristwatch had been a gift from my soon-to-be ex-wife for our twentieth anniversary. I had taken us both on a cruise-ship in the Mediterranean and this was her anniversary gift to me. The potential negative connotations are temporarily pushed aside as I cling onto it in hope.

Robert had offered to have the battery replaced on numerous occasions, but I couldn't bring myself to take the watch off so that he could do it. The hour and minute hands had stopped at about 11:45 and I hear the song from my childhood playing repeatedly in my head:

"…and the clock
stopped,
never to go again
when the old man died!"

How macabre; but I honestly think there is a strong possibility this is going to happen. That I am going to die.

Of all the things most valuable to me in Helen Joseph—other than my sanity, which is by now bolting out of the room—the one thing worth stealing remained firmly attached to my wrist. Yet no-one attempted to steal it.

I find this very peculiar, as when one is in an abnormal state and environment then 'normality' seems to be unusual. It seemed normal to me that someone would want to steal it.

A voice summons me from down the cold corridor and into a separate room that is usually locked to the patients. A group of official-looking people had arrived earlier on and I have noticed individual patients being led into the room intermittently. It is my turn, and I am ushered down the passage. Inside, I find a panel of about five doctors and psychiatrists, including Doctor Know-it-all, seated around a large table in the centre of the room. On the one hand, it is a relief to see so many intelligent-looking faces staring back at me—and I mean STARING! On the other hand, I am painfully aware that I am being scrutinised.

The challenge suddenly strikes me; I must try and convince the faces-that-stare that I am okay, but really at the same time, I struggle to believe this myself.

I must fight and pretend that all is good, convincing them that I am stable, that I am showing potential, and have all intention to comply with medication as well as a progression towards healing. Basically, I have to convince them that I will comply with their directions. I HAVE TO OBEY.

The panel scrutinizes me and asks probing questions to ascertain just how far I am from the edge. Their unheard thoughts permeate the room and my mind...

"Should he be permanently sectioned?"

"Should he be placed in assisted living?"

"Should he be discharged and allowed to go back home?"

"Should he be discharged and sent back to another psychiatric institution, and if so, for how long?"

Everything is still hazy, but I try to be positive and fight through the fog.

After several probing questions, I stand up and explain to the panel with the faces-that-stare, "My left foot is still limp, and I can't walk properly... Look." I demonstrate a few hobbled steps to visually reinforce my claim.

"I believe it's a side-effect of the Seroquel," I explain with authority, fully convinced they will see my point.

The head psychiatrist looks down her nose at me with disdain and fobs me off with, "I get the feeling you will blame any and every symptom on the medication!"

So, here I am once again, trapped between the medicine and the deep blue sea. The faces-that-stare don't buy into my theory. I am the patient and they are learned, you see.

Pressing home the concept that I am not insane, I utilize the anatomical terms for the specific muscles I believe are the problem. "Doctor, it feels like the tibialis anterior is lame. Look how, when I place the weight on my heel, the front of the foot drops down!"

My anatomy and physiology courses at university give me the confidence to feel that I am showing knowledge and logic. They MUST SURELY see I am in control of my senses. Yet, they still don't buy it. There is no place in their precious medication for a 'drop-foot' side-effect. That is just NOT possible!

The psychiatric fraternity appears to do the utmost to remove the blame from the medication and transfer it to the patient's state of mind. They look at the symptoms they want to see and then refer to the diagnostic guidelines, branding you with the most appropriate disorder they can find, so that they can throw a pill at you! The medicine can't be wrong; the medicine will heal you! Because, remember, they can NEVER be wrong!

The symptoms I present are ascribed to 'Borderline Personality Disorder'! The medicine dampens my emotions, and brutally chokes back any tears as I am branded with a disorder once again.

Staring in resigned acceptance, I wait for them to tell me how they are going to continue controlling my life—for now, at least. They dismiss me and send me back to the fruitcake bakery once again—not sure when or if I am going to have a reprieve of any sort. I leave behind the faces-that-stare on the wooden chairs at the wooden table with their stubborn minds to decide on my fate and life once again! They still control my power.

Supper time arrives once again, and we file into the mess hall on cue, hoping for the best.

The Baritone brigade bay aloud from the smoking lounge, reminding me rudely of where I am. It is *One Flew over the Cuckoo's Nest* but with an unpaid, lousier cast.

Every day is Groundhog Day.

SMALL TREASURES

Jackie had understandably not allowed my children to come and visit me in Helen Joseph hospital, but she, herself arrived a number of times. My children would have broken down, as they could never have coped with seeing me in THAT state and in THAT institution.

My sister Kim visited me regularly and fought like a Trojan for me throughout the experience. They brought all sorts of treasures that were imported from the normal world. Chocolate, Coca-Cola, and biscuits, all sweet things. That was okay, as my body craved sugar—or sustenance in any form for that matter. There was dried fruit and biltong, most of which I ate during the visit and sent the rest back from whence it came. I never kept any of that as it would have been stolen.

I sucked up as much nutrition as I could in that short hour so as to bolster the empty, lost shell of a body I still lived in. We had been told by counsellors not to take too much sugar as it caused a sugar spike. This sugar spike was apparently not good for you if you were on medication.

"Living is bad for me ON the medication!"

I resisted the temptation of the sweet food for as long as I could. Once tasted though, I would finish a whole chocolate bar with relish. My body needed the sustenance, yet my mind resisted it. Sugar-spike or not, it tasted damn fine! As we sit in the visitor's space one afternoon, Klepto-Number-One sidles up to us in his mistaken stealth. His crab-like sideways shuffle leaves no-one under any impression that his intentions aren't shady. He stares and stalks us as he tries to coax some of the luxurious food from me and my visitor. We look askance at him, all the while trying not to make eye contact as that will be his cue to intrude and ask for something. He is always a threat and I never feel safe in that unit. Ever.

In that emaciated state, I occasionally wonder what will happen if anyone attacks me physically. At the time, I looked extremely vulnerable, but had over twelve years of martial arts training amassed two black belts in different styles. This made me not only capable of defending myself, but also of doing serious damage to an attacker; BUT this was NOT advisable in a psychiatric ward!

There are two aspects of relevance here ... One was that I was still able to weigh up the pros and cons of the situation, and the other was that I had demonstrated self-restraint. It was an unknowingly positive sign.

We theoretically marry with the commitment of 'until death do us part', and at times at Helen Joseph, I felt this could be the fulfilment of that promise made so many years ago in front of friends and family. I didn't want to, but I still felt it was a strong possibility I might die.

Suicide was never an option to me, yet I now understand how low one can feel when depressed or showing side-effects of anti-depressants or withdrawal. I am too damn scared that it might hurt like hell just before I go!

Uneven thuds echo on the odd occasion I try to run

down the passage, but my left foot falls down with a dead flop and I keep twisting my ankle, so I stop trying. I start to believe I will never walk properly again as the 'drop-foot' has lasted for weeks —possibly even months — by now.

The fearful, drugged haze continues unabated as the new regime takes over from the withdrawals from the previous pills. I still have bad anxiety and my fingers shake constantly like that of an alcoholic. When I point this out to the psychiatrist, she responds that it is due to the "deep-seated anxiety".

I have no energy and my heart pounds in inconsistent palpitations. It is very difficult for me to pinpoint these as side-effects of the medication I am on, or withdrawal symptoms from the medication that I used before, but I know it has to be one of the causes.

People continue to try and befriend me, and I always refuse. All I want is to just get out of this place and go home, but I am not allowed to leave until after the five days 'observation' are over; all the time, never knowing what will happen to me afterward, or where I will be going. In my mind, I had 'failed the test' set by the 'people-that-stare' and the mental torture would continue. It was just a case of where I would be living when the torture continued.

THE REPRIEVE

Unexpectedly, at the end of the five days, I am

summoned to the nurse's station.

"You are being discharged to go back to Butterfly Lodge," she announces.

"Butterfly Lodge!?"

"I thought I couldn't go back there?" I whisper.

"Well, your family has arranged it for you," the nurse in charge mumbles.

I was under the impression that they didn't want me at Butterfly Lodge ever again. This was not ideally what I wanted; I wanted to be with my children. However, I accept this as a second-best option and at least get out of 'Hell'en-on-Earth'.

THE ESIDIMENI TRAGEDY

During this time, an immense tragedy unfolded but it failed to reach the South African news yet. The state-sponsored psychiatric hospital chain known as Life Esidimeni had decided to transport hundreds of patients to other outsourced and apparently approved facilities.

Due to maladministration and fraud of the South African Health Department, many of the facilities had not been legally vetted and had obtained licences illegally.

In the transportation process, 140 patients had died due to mistreatment and malnutrition!

I was one of the lucky people that had fallen outside of that group, due mainly to luck, finance, and family support. It was a massive crime against humanity and to this day, no true responsibility has been taken.

I think about those poor people and what they must have gone through. The fear and lack of correct medication and procedure must have been traumatic. Many of these people would not have known about side-effects, withdrawal symptoms, or inter-dose withdrawals. They wouldn't have had the education or knowledge to question the authority of the medical staff or institutions that ruled them. They would have been forced to go along with chaotic instructions, and fear of not knowing where they were going or what was happening to them. They would have been shoved, pulled, ignored, and cajoled into doing what the staff wanted them to do. They would have all stared fear in the face with some taken permanently away from their family and friends.

This occurrence is sadly symptomatic of the way psychiatric patients are too often looked at. Stuck with the stigma of the 'madness' of being mentally ill. To be ignored and waved away with a disdainful "He/she is just crazy, anyway".

BACK TO BUTTERFLY LODGE

It is late afternoon, five days after my admission, when Jackie comes to fetch me. This is a massive surprise to me, as she had endorsed the initial trip to Helen Joseph and had been one of the signatories allowing me to be sectioned.

I change out of the state-issued sweat suit and pull on the same jeans and blood-stained t-shirt I had removed five days previously. The blood is now dry and caked hard, but once again, I don't care. At least I am getting out of this shit-hole! There are no farewells for any of the patients or for the nurses as I had forged no relationships whilst there, and there is no need for any polite greetings.

The clothes still hang off me as I tighten my belt to its last hole in a desperate attempt to keep my trousers up. Each hole in the belt had been utilised independently over the last few months as the belt drew tighter and tighter whilst the weight progressively dropped off. It is a stark reminder of what had become of my previously strong, fit body.

There is a strange connection and atmosphere

between me and Jackie as the love is clearly gone; it is replaced by an awkwardness between us. Stilted conversation and anxious silent moments accompany us as we walk to the parking lot where her car sits under a lone security light. We stop briefly next to her car and Jackie takes out her cellular phone to take a picture of me, saying, "This is for you as a reminder of what you looked like when you were sick."

I don't argue, yet feel sheepishly ashamed as I know I look like shit and am not proud of it, but it is definitely beyond my control at this point. I now hate the passenger seat next to the driver's side as I know its space has been replaced by another man that had played a part of the demise of my family unit. I now had to temporarily sit where his cheating arse often found a place.

On the way back to Butterfly Lodge, I try my best to get her to drop me off at the children's new home which they had moved into while I was away.

"Can't you take me to them?" I plead powerlessly, aware that I am still at the mercy of others.

"Absolutely not. No way," is the cruel retort.

As we arrive outside the entrance to Butterfly Lodge for the second stint, the phone rings in the car. She answers and I hear the voice of her father come through the speaker. He is confirming arrangements for that evening.

Upon hearing his voice, the tears start to flow down my cheeks. Having lost my father to cancer several years before, this was a man who I had learnt to love as a father-in-law and had not heard his voice in at least five months. The deep timbre of his baritone voice claws the emotion from inside my soul as I contemplate how THAT relationship is in effect all over as well. This was another unknown consequence of infidelity and divorce and adds to the collateral damage. On the up side, at least there was some emotion lurking deep down in there inside of me, subdued and numbed still by sadness and medication.

Stalling Jackie in the car outside Butterfly Lodge, I attempt to delay the inevitable re-admission. It works for a few minutes until she becomes agitated and drives through the entrance and into the small, but peaceful parking area under the trees. Alighting from the car, I slowly shuffle along with Jackie in tow and reluctantly step across the threshold and back into the office at Butterfly Lodge. All the other patients have already gone to bed, and as we sit down around the office table with the manager, a night security orderly strategically keeps an eye nearby.

The manager reads me the riot act. "We have reluctantly agreed to re-admit you as there had been no rooms available at Tara Psychiatric Hospital and your family has promised that you would conform to the rules. Do you agree?"

"Yes. I agree" I sheepishly respond, not completely convinced by my own reply.

She continues, "If you break any of the rules, you will be sectioned again and sent to Tara hospital!"

I am shit-scared of that possibility. In fact, I am fearful of ANY hospital of that ilk. Both of the names 'Tara' and 'Weskoppies' hold an inordinate amount of fear and for me as they signify a 'point-of-no-return' —a place that if I were to be admitted, I would never leave again.

"You also undertake to stick to the medicine the doctor has prescribed!"

"Yes, I will take the medicine," I sigh. Trapped again, I must conform, all the while knowing this is bad for me. After the fear-inducing lecture, I go to the kitchen and eat some supper left over from the earlier meal, take the prescribed medicine meekly, and go to bed.

Jackie's new life without me continues as she pops off to a family dinner with her parents.

Leaving through the office doorway, I can see the disapproval in her eyes. The look in them had long ago changed from loving empathy to absolute disdain.

I don't recognise the person behind those eyes that had resided there for so long. Another person that had no heart inhabited her skin and this makes it easier for me to fall out of love with her. There had been a quantum shift in the person I once knew, and this makes it easier for me ultimately to forget her. The person I had been married to was dead, but her ghost still haunted my earth.

--- --- ---

Ironically, I continue to break rules as I know I can't stick to them all, but I do so in a gentle way as a form of peaceful protest.

The return made Butterfly Lodge seem once again

like a paradise. I contrasted the garden and swimming pool with the vinyl floors and dirty bath of Helen Joseph. The food was still excellent, and the room had 'only' three beds.

It is clean and we even have our own shower and a toilet that works. I am happy to place my bum on this one! After all, I HAD been scraping the bottom of the proverbial barrel at Helen Joseph!

There were a few wooden cabins on the grounds of Butterfly Lodge. These wooden cabins were allocated to individuals who had been assigned 'assisted living' status. The cabins were very simple and measured only about 4-by-4 metres, yet to me, these cabins start to resemble a five-star resort. The people in these cabins have their own space with their own beds and a television for one! I continue to see the possibility that this might be my fate from here-on in... assisted living in a clinic.

Although I still have that dark, high, wide wall in front of me and have never had to live in such a space since the days of military conscription, it feels a whole lot better than Helen Joseph hospital. It's all a matter of comparison, I guess.

Another contracted psychiatrist continues to prescribe the Fluoxetine, that was by now on a very short medicine list. As always, I was extremely reluctant to take an anti-depressant knowing full well how the Serlife and Serdep (Zoloft) had affected me. However, I was compelled to take it, understanding full well the negative consequences. So, I capitulated simultaneously asking her, "Doctor, please reduce the dose of Seroquel to 150mg as I can't walk straight at night on 200mg?"

The 200mg dose gave me an impossibly dry mouth, causing me to stumble and fall against the walls like a drunk. Fortunately for me, she listens and reduces it to 150mg saying, "Please stick rigidly to this, and let me know how it goes."

The reduction of the dose results in less drowsiness and my walking improves. My sleep improves a bit as well, although I continue to have vivid dreams and am very drained in the morning when I awake.

Butterfly Lodge nurse's report:

"Sleeps well. No complaints. He spends most of the day alone, attends sessions, takes his meds well, but has difficulty in waking up in the morning." I had very little difficulty waking up, but it was rather 'getting up'.

NOTES AND THINGS

"Please remember to submit your diaries to the office by Thursday the latest," is the weekly and almost daily instruction. All patients—or 'clients' as the staff preferred to call us at Butterfly Lodge—had to keep a diary with their thoughts and feelings written down. This was so that the counsellors could read them and notice any potential problems, issues, or progress in the writer.

"If you don't hand in a completed diary on Thursday, you will forfeit the right of going shopping on Saturday morning." Shopping was a very welcome outing for most and a relaxed change to the routine of the week.

Everyone mumbles in agreement, except me. I didn't want to shop anyway, so I refuse to write in the diary. NOT...ONE...WORD. It seems so pointless, and I don't want strangers reading my thoughts; they are mine and mine alone and are to be shared only if I care to.

As much as I didn't want to write, I also didn't want to read. I still couldn't. My mind was still stuttering along, trying to deal with unsorted issues. There were too many thoughts cluttering my head and I couldn't find the one, first issue to attack and break the impasse.

I was still toiling with withdrawal effects from older medicine and trying to adapt to new prescriptions that had been forced on me at Helen Joseph.

Every Saturday after check-in, I would uncaringly watch the 'diarists' go shopping in all their fineness. They would excitedly dress up a bit smarter than normal and check their wallets to see if their management-limited budget would allow them to buy what they wanted. Chattering happily away, they traipse to the minivan driven by the always-bombastic John. I am not allowed go with, which is fine as normality is anathema to me.

The two-hour shopping expedition passes by in a flash and they all return babbling away, seemingly more positive about life. Disembarking from the mini-bus, they stride into the living area or to their rooms to continue the weekend activities. And once again, I watch the process unfold. Just sit and watch, all the time trying to make sense of my life and predicament.

The next day, being a Sunday, is visitor's day and guests can visit from 2:00pm until 4:00pm. I initially dread it. The people I loved were coming to visit and share their love and concern with me. I wanted them to be well, but I would stress out unbearably before they arrived. Peculiarly, I would sometimes be relieved if they didn't make it; I wanted them to be there, but then again not. I couldn't communicate properly anyway, and hadn't formulated a path out of the hell in my mind yet. Knowing all this, I was painfully aware of the effect it was having on my family.

Yet, I continued.

Fearfully at 2:00 in the afternoon, I hear my family arrive to help boost me and themselves, if I am willing or able. There is no logic in this fear of course, yet I stay in my room as before, awaiting their arrival.

The voices arrive once again, alive with hope for progress in order to substantiate their wilting faith in me. They are cautious and unbelievably positive in their approach, considering there has been no progress for five months.

I was the willow tree, bowed and fragile with my many fronds gently and feebly swaying to the wind, hanging over the stream of life as it trickled by. Relying on the sustenance from the soil and water below, but not quite reaching into the pools of joy that are so tantalisingly close. My family gently and joyfully swing on the fronds as they tug me closer to the stream, but cannot quite get me to draw the life-giving water from it.

For me to break through, my fronds must grow a little bit more. They must be guided from without, with the fronds gently brushing the surface and within, until the roots reach out to sip the water of life when my growth toward healing would again take hold and accelerate forward.

I nevertheless venture out of my room in cautious anticipation, like the other patients. Only once someone has made their way across the garden and entered through the door of my room, do I look up and reluctantly greet them. Feeling embarrassed again by the lack of progress, and aware of the pointlessness of remaining in my room, I follow them to a more private spot outside. Finding a place under the trees, they talk with controlled and calculated animation as they attempt to draw me out of my silent sadness.

Lisa has brought card games to try and entice me out of the cracks in the floor where I try and hide from the world. Initially, it doesn't work. Nothing works, yet my people try and try and try. They put on happy faces and hold back tears to protect me.

Yet, I am still stuck.

> A heart taken by love
> Nurtured to fulfilment
> Then at once
> Drained of all substance
> Meaning and family questioned
> Words are replaced by an emotional vacuum
> Breathe in
> But can't breathe out

Happiness deserted for a while
Where do we find it again?
The innocent ones that bind us are still there
Stitching the torn tapestry
With inexperienced hands and minds
As the winds of change keep tugging and tearing it apart
Again!
They too clinging onto hope against hope
For life's positive intervention
But where is it?
When will their hero return?
Slowly

—*Craig Dawtrey*

WALKING WITH DEE

A full six weeks into my stay, I overhear a conversation outside near the administration office. The driver for the clients at Butterfly Lodge (John-the-noxious), has returned from collecting a new patient from the O.R. Tambo International Airport in Johannesburg. This is no more significant than any other arrival. People came and left on a weekly basis anyway as they evaded, faked, or achieved recovery. I get on with my doing nothing, but ruminating against all advice, still trying to see a sliver of light and hope.

Sitting on my small patio later in the day, I notice

a very tall lady join us. She doesn't just arrive, but changes the atmosphere as she glides in on long strides, her shining hair glistening in the late winter sun. Six-feet tall in the old measurements, and fitting the description of elegance, it is impossible not to notice her.

In true form, I sit. And observe. And worry. And analyse. And criticize in my own head. And scheme. And appreciate.

Later, as most polite people do, the lady sweeps past and greets me. "Hi, my name is Dee."

I growl out some nocturnal, guttural semblance of a greeting that is akin to a Neanderthal on a hunting expedition, but with less grace than that now-extinct species. Looking the part, I had not cut what little hair I had or shaved for weeks, and the grey, matted hair on my head and face made me look like the hobo I was so afraid of becoming.

Yet, she smiles. A lady has made conversation with me. She is seemingly not repulsed or fearful of the person I have become and present to her on first impression. She merely identified with another tortured person that was going through some issues like her. Albeit one sided, this beautiful-natured person tries to make friends with a dark, sad apparition. And the apparition sits, as he tries to interpret what he is observing.

Sitting within my own body and mind that has no congruence is disconcerting for me, but I am intensely aware that I must tone it down to my own level of understanding. Dee looks like she is on a vacation. She is at a coastal Bohemia, and I am one of the observers wondering, "What does someone like this do here?"

She is beautifully groomed with long brown hair and a slight tan on her skin from the earlier visit to Cape Town. Wearing a brightly-coloured short summer dress, flat sandals protect her feet, and dark glasses shade her eyes on her pretty face.

The following Sunday, my brother-in-law, Brad, joins the rest of my family. Tilting his head in Dee's direction, he teases me with a, "Craig, why don't you get the number of that babe with the long legs?"

"I am not interested," is my asthmatic answer.

"Come on, Craig, what's the matter with you?" continues Brad.

"I can't," I plead.

I am not in any frame of mind for a relationship of any kind and I know I look like shit. I am no example of a virile confident man, being painfully aware that I am certainly no catch at this point. As I was to share the house with her for the next few weeks, I nonetheless have no need for her number. Dee was to play a huge part on my healing journey in the weeks to come, but at this stage, I have no idea.

Dee had been struggling with her own demons for years, although at the time, I had no idea to what extent or what they may have entailed. Everyone at Butterfly Lodge was there for a reason, and never really for good ones. They were there to try and find a way forward and out of their specific mental prison. Everyone there was tormented to some greater or lesser extent.

It was just the nature of the beast and we all resided

in its corpulent, gluttonous belly. The beast, called life, would beat its victim down at will and toy with its emotions. Once done, it would simply devour as much as it wanted. Now and again, it would purge itself by vomiting up a wretched soul it had grown tired of and leave its remains to take care of itself. I was not in the space to concern myself with other people's issues at this stage, as I was still selfishly interred in my own mind's problems.

Dee would partake in all the facility's organised activities as she tried to rid herself of the wounds that had shattered her gentle self. She would painstakingly and with attentive perfection complete all the art tasks. Her attention to detail, colour, and precision strike me even in my haze. I mentioned my observation of this precision to her when I had broken through and started bonding with her later.

"You really are a perfectionist, Dee. Never going over the lines, consistent colour, always closing off the ends of the neat swirls or circles on pages that never have 'dog-ears' on the corners."

"Thanks, Craig, but I am certainly far from perfect," she replies shyly.

Unexpectedly one day, one of the first things I say to her is, "You have lovely feet!"

"Really? I have never noticed," she says glancing down at the floor. "Thank you."

"You are welcome," I croak with a half-smile, wondering if I have seen this because I am always looking down at the floor, pondering and searching for the road out of my hell. Or is it because they were attached to her tanned legs? I toil with the quandary and settle on the second probability.

TREADING WATER

It was nearing the southern hemisphere spring of 2016, and still very chilly at night and in the early morning; yet, people who weren't afraid of the water or the South African sun would congregate around the swimming pool and sunbathe. I had always been a keen swimmer and quite a water baby, yet I was still averse to its touch.

For a full year, I had never ventured to place my foot in the water at the ocean or in my swimming pool at home. The same applied here. Others do. They swim. They splash as they laugh at the challenge of the cold spring water. Once again, I wonder if I will ever feel the need for the splash of cool, soothing water on my body or the gentle massage of beach sand under my bare feet.

There is a skylight in my room that is made from a green plastic material, which is very efficient in bringing light into the room. It is also a great sundial. As the season moves on, I can tell the time by the movement of the green glow. When the cream-soda warmth hits my face, I know I am late for schedule and in trouble! It is Nature's efficiency. Ignore her at your own peril as she will always win. Carpe a.m.

And so, the new season spies on me. Spring stalks me as it brings its change. It feels like an intruder to my isolation, unwelcomingly forcing its way into my life. Realising that I have remained stagnant for two seasons, bordering on a whole year and feeling I have not moved forward in any way at all, is a daunting experience. I start smelling the change in the seasons. Moisture seeps into the room and taps me on the shoulder as spring blossom scents tantalise and tease my nose.

Having lived on the South African Highveld my whole life, I recognize a Highveld thunderstorm's approach merely by the change in the air pressure and light. The cumulus clouds that creep in from the south-western sky slowly blanket the city-scape and with their grey and then black, bruised faces drop their, at first gentle, brief showers. From a distance they growl as they announce their seasonal arrival. These clouds grew over days and weeks whilst lifting their hunched backs upward, shouting down at the earth as bigger drops fall, soaking the ground and bringing relieved smiles. The trees and plants release their seasonal wintry grasp on their blossoms and permit them to see the sun for the first time. Like Pavlov's dog, the patterns of consistency in nature creep into every aspect of my day.

The summer birds that had migrated for the winter start returning as the vegetation proliferates and brings seeds for them to eat. Once again, I observe how territorial the birds are, as the same ones leave the nests at sunrise and then return at sunset. The same number and species of birds fly in the same direction every morning and then every evening return to the place from whence they had come.

As darkness falls on clear evenings, I stare up at the sky and watch as the moon waxes and wanes and in its lunar wake drags a planet behind as it shows the way towards dawn. Disappearing over the horizon, another planet brightly announces its presence as they switch places in the city sky.

"What are you looking at, Craig?" Dee asks.

"The stars and the planets, Dee."

"How can you tell the difference between the two?"

"Well, you see, the stars are scattered all about the sky and they sparkle. This is because they generate their own light and are effectively suns."

"Okay, Craig, and the planets?"

"Well, the planets follow a very clear path in the sky, called the Ecliptic, and will always be found in that arc. They change positions throughout the year as they revolve around the sun along the Ecliptic. So, you never have to scan the sky for the planets. Secondly the planets don't flicker. They glow with the calm reflection of the sun that lights our solar system."

"Oh, Craig, that's awesome!"

We stare at the sky and find Jupiter and Venus along with some temporary peace.

NOLEEN

The first swimmer of the season is Noleen. She is a short, strongly built woman in her late forties. She had, in a moment of frustrated desire for change, cut her hair very short and then dyed it a shocking pink, which lightens up the austere look it threatened to create. She walks around the facility religiously like a Muslim on the Hajj to Mecca. She does it with a scowl and a purpose.

None of the other patients knew it at first, but she was an incredibly talented artist who had beautiful paintings on show at a national gallery in Johannesburg. It all becomes evident when, in a positive moment she opens her door and starts doing her art again near her room. Her easel makes its way into the gentle spring sun outside near the kitchen as she settles down in front of it. Her rainbow-coloured pastel crayons rest comfortably in trained hands as she brings life to the bland canvas and colour into our lives. Her newly-revealed creativity gives us a shared pride. One of 'ours' is so talented! It is our home after all during the recovery period, and we always try to assist each other in our own way; sometimes intentionally, and other times without being aware we are doing so. We are our own in-house support group.

Noleen doesn't like to be greeted in the morning unless she allows you to come into her personal space. But still, she strides around the vast lands of Pine Avenue on a daily basis. She swims with intent. She sun-bathes. She paints. And occasionally, she joins us at the dinner table. She chats to Dee, or Dee chats to her (Dee chats to anyone, as she has a very gentle heart and is concerned about their wellbeing).

Noleen is angry, and understandably so. The medicine regime isn't helping at all, and there seems to be no break from the darkness for her.

And one day she died. It was that abrupt!

I am so glad I wasn't there when she passed away, as I had left Butterfly Lodge in order to try my stint at a normal life again. Noleen was not able to breach the boundaries back from the brink and despair of depression. One of the symptoms she had complained of could be diagnosed as *Post-SSRI Sexual Dysfunction (PSSD) or Persistent Genital Arousal Disorder (PGAD)*.

> "People with this condition become sexually aroused without any sexual activity or stimulation even when there's no reason to feel sexually aroused. PGAD can last for hours, days or weeks at a time and can be disruptive to one's life."
>
> —*Healthline*

Noleen had mentioned this endlessly debilitating aroused state to Dee in a personal discussion, yet, I have no idea if those symptoms had ceased at the time of her death.

To our dismay, she overdosed while still in recovery. She had, over many years, been prescribed numerous drugs in order to help her situation, with none of them seeming to work. I do recall her complaining about horrendous side-effects that she couldn't cope with.

Whilst I was still a client at Butterfly Lodge, she had asked me for advice on how to move forward as I had at that stage made such progress that I was seen as an example for other patients there. Sadly, I couldn't show her the way. No one could.

I suspect no one can, as one needs to see this light ultimately for oneself in order to move forward. All the people and the group around you as a patient are there for support and guidance, but the change starts within yourself and that first step. You need to find your own way, and if you are fortunate enough, you will have family and or friends to help and guide you. If not, you can become a statistic. A percentage. A victim of life's challenges, or psychiatry at its experimental ground zero.

Goodbye, Noleen.

WHEN WATER HEALED ITSELF

And so the swallows would venture out again every day
With their unbridled enthusiasm
They sought sustenance for their young
They gently threw their souls
With their vulnerable bodies out of the nests
And soared upon helpful breezes
As they searched for what they trusted as natural
Gravity tugged them down
Yet they knew their wings
Would lift them away from what lay below
They were assured to return

And give the bounty to their young
For that is how life was
It would deliver what was worked for
The swallows swooped
And they bounced off the water as they sipped
A temporary gash in the surface of the lake hinted at their cursory visit
The lake healed almost instantaneously
As another bird dipped in briefly to sip and then left
We humans swoop in
And take from what lies there
Once we have left though
The scars lay open
The water does not close
Sometimes it freezes
Only to leave the watery memory
To struggle as it thaws and hopefully
Gently releases its grasp on our souls
Once spring breathes a breath of hope and life into the lake
The reflection of the new face of happiness
Might replace what winter scarred her with
Yet we take another
And again

—Craig Dawtrey

ANOTHER MARK

Mark. God, how I hate that name. I associate it with the break-up of my marriage as well as my family unit and as such, everything negative with it.

Life in all its self-centred frivolity sent me not a lifeline, but a room-mate called Mark!

He is much younger than me, and had survived multiple traumatic events prior to my arrival. A failed suicide attempt—where he had apparently jumped off a building—has left him with a speech impediment and some facial disfigurement.

He had been medicated for years prior to his admission to Butterfly Lodge, and this is not his first stay at the facility. He has a very gentle way about him, and always has sweets and chocolates with him that he willingly shares with anyone who cares to have.

He is back at Butterfly Lodge after a few months away; he was sectioned to another harsher mental institution due to some psychiatric rule infringement. For the first few weeks, he has a room to himself. I am happy with that arrangement, as I already have two young lads sharing the room with me that have substance-recovery challenges and I certainly don't need or want another room-mate.

One of my room-mates had completed his sixty-day stay, and duly graduated from the facility, allowing a bed-space to open in my room. In all management's wisdom, they decide to place Mark with me and my other young room-mate.

Having no say in the matter, I wince in mute acceptance.

All I wanted was people who don't eat potato crisps and sweets in the room, or smoke outside my bedroom window late at night when Doctor Seroquel was making me drowsy.

The new main house has a lovely, warm television lounge in which the patients congregate to watch movies after taking evening medication. An 8 p.m. bell rings, and we would stand in a queue waiting to have pills thrust at us by Sister Seko. She has a friendly face and a very positive disposition, and her constantly smiling face and bright way lifts me ever-so-slightly within the constraints imposed on my medicated mind. Once the pills have been taken, we need to sign the medicine register, confirming we have done as required. This is another regime that freaks me out.

Relatively soon after my release from Helen Joseph's not-so-gentle bosom, with the medication taken, two sandwiches with peanut-butter and honey under the belt, and a movie completed, I retire to bed. As I walk past the kitchen and glance to my right through the open kitchen door, I notice Mark at the kitchen table. He sits on a chair adjacent to it and seems to be doing sit-ups. I think to myself that this is rather strange at 10:00 at night in the kitchen, but hey, we are in a psychiatric recovery unit anyway, so anything is possible.

He looks a bit odd and I notice his abdominal muscles appear particularly weak as he seems to be lying a bit too far back, not completing the movement according to my trained satisfaction. The fact that he has half a sandwich in his hand and the other half in his mouth makes me debate the validity of what I am seeing. Is this the epitome of the 'one sandwich short of a picnic' scenario? I decide I should check up on him.

"Please help me," he slurs and I realise this is not a voluntary gym workout, but clearly the lad is in trouble. Rapidly entering the kitchen, I try to assist in getting him into a seated position, ensuring I don't get any half-chewed food on my hands.

I notice that his back muscles must be in spasm, as he can't maintain the seated position. There is a terrible look of desperation and fear in his eyes and he lies back again as his contracting muscles arch and pull.

Fuck, what now? I think. Responsibility for others is something I am not ready for, but hey, here I am! Talk about being thrown in at the deep end!

I hurriedly summon the night nurse who gawks wide-eyed at the situation, like a man who has just had his prostate examined. Night-shift for her was for snoozing and late-night peanut-butter and honey sandwiches—not overdosed, distressed boys!

Not wanting to stay, and frankly not having the knowledge to assist any further, I leave her and the night manager to sort the issue out. The inevitable flow of curious onlookers traipses quizzically past with the reaction turning to shock when the ambulance comes to collect him a few minutes later. It is incredibly daunting to see someone being carried out on a stretcher—after socialising with you only a few hours before—not sure if they are alive or in the process of dying.

Watching the white ambulance leave with Mark, its emergency light alternately shares its red glow with the walls and plants as it slowly reverses down the driveway. There is something about an ambulance arriving at your abode that I am convinced deters anyone that is of moderately sober mind from doing anything self-destructive.

Every time I heard an ambulance or other siren, I was terrified it was coming to collect me to take me to Tara Psychiatric Hospital, as I was under the impression that that possibility was still on the table, and that I was still sectioned.

Still in slight medication-reduced shock, I trundle the short fifteen or so metres across the garden next to the swimming pool and back to my room, where I seek solace from sleep in bed.

The next morning light and check-in brings us the news on Mark and what had apparently happened. Mark had smuggled alcohol into his room after a day out with his mother, and made a barbiturate cocktail with a twist of prescribed medicine. Whether this overdose was an intentional suicide attempt or merely a case of over-indulgence, none of us will ever know. I will never see sit-ups the same way ever again, especially if they are performed in the kitchen.

After a few days, the issue is discussed with the other patients at Butterfly Lodge. We are informed that Mark is returning and we should try and make him feel welcome. There is no judgement from the others, just a caring concern and voicing of support. Anyone who needs trauma counselling will have it made available to them. I don't need it as my emotions are still numbed by the medication.

Some weeks later, after Sunday visitors have left, I see Mark asleep on his bed in our room.

Approaching him gingerly, I am cautious not to awaken him. As he lies on his back, I notice he has wet his trousers.

"Mark, can you hear me?" I enquire—no response.

"Mark!" shaking him

A gurgled, "Mmmmm" is all that comes from his pursed mouth.

Checking his breathing and pulse, I realise he is unconscious, yet thankfully, still alive.

"Please, we need the nurse!" urgently this time.

He is taken once again to a hospital where the staff perform a stomach-pump and he returns a few days later, apparently none the worse-for-wear.

It only came to me a bit after that incident, that I HAD to be improving, as I was making sensible, logical decisions that required intellectual application. The events at Butterfly Lodge were starting to force me forward in a positive direction, even though I was unaware of it at that point. Wow! Was this possibly progress?

HEKSIE AND KARLIEN

The unlikely partnership of Afrikaans Boere-diva and street-special hound had found its way into our lives shortly after I originally checked into Butterfly Lodge. Karlien is an Afrikaans-speaking lady of about sixty years of age. She dresses impeccably every day, and takes great attention to her make-up and clothes. She is an immensely proud, tall woman with blonde hair. Karlien's husband had passed away relatively recently. Along with depression caused by her husband's death and the loss of her previous family life, she had experienced rejection from the balance of her family. Her favourite day is definitely Saturday, thanks to the morning shopping spree.

Her beautifully ugly dog, Heksie (Witchy), is her dedicated friend and companion. Heksie is a medium-sized mixed breed with scruffy sand-coloured wire-textured hair and friendly, gentle brown eyes. Heksie is one of the first characters awake each morning and shows an enthusiasm way beyond her looks.

She greets everyone at any time of the day, including me. Initially, I have no affection for the dog, but after a while I start responding to Heksie's attention-seeking, despite her penchant for rolling in the dirt as well as her shit, occasionally. She follows this rolling regime by joining the group during many therapies. She enthusiastically comes into the therapy rooms and independently greets each person in turn, where the human response to her will depend on what she smells of! After her round of greetings, she lies down and watches as the humans go about their daily activities.

I eventually take a liking to the dog and her scruffy enthusiasm, and start playing with her outside in the garden. Realising she doesn't get much exercise —and for a dog this is fun —it becomes fun for me as well.

The theory at Butterfly Lodge of allowing pets to

join the patients was a good idea it seemed, as it allows for the no-obligation and non-judgmental interaction from animal to human and then back again.

The 'doggie-therapy' gets me to smile a bit more, and eventually, I start to laugh. We ultimately become quite attached to each other, and she knows I will play with her in the late afternoons, actively searching and singling me out.

It is a late afternoon, and I am sitting outside my room on the little patio when I happen to glance up and see a person stumbling across the walkway not fifteen metres from me. Taking a while to make sense of the scene —and after initially not understanding what is happening —I pick up that something is clearly wrong with what I am seeing.

The figure is that of Karlien. She is dressed only in panty-hose, panties, and a shirt as she stumbles and crawls across the floor, dangerously close to the swimming pool. Appearing oblivious to what is happening, she is clearly intoxicated by something. I stay seated, rooted to the chair. What am I to do?

Fortunately, one of the care-givers notices the goings-on simultaneously and hurriedly approaches her to assist.

They help her to lie down and cover her with a blanket to restore her temporarily misplaced dignity. She is whisked away to hospital, and treated for the overdose.

One might wonder how a patient overdoses in a medically-controlled environment where access to prescribed drugs is strictly controlled. Well, some of the overdosing cases I observed whilst in these facilities, are precipitated by patients that pretend to take their medicine for a few days, and then, once they have accumulated a large quantity of their pills, they simultaneously take the whole lot. Some survive unscathed, others are permanently scarred, and sadly, some die.

Upon Karlien's return, I start talking to her a bit more, thanks to the shared relationship with Heksie. As I am fluent in Afrikaans and have started to come out of the closed state I have been in for so long, we talk to each other in her home language. Due to the nature of the facility we are in, as well as the type of treatment we are undergoing there, the discussion varies from how we are feeling, what we think of others in the facility, what medication we are taking, and even the colour of our urine. Well, we had to be sure our kidneys were working fine, didn't we? She takes much solace and joy in watching me bring a side of Heksie's playful personality out that she has never been aware of. It is good for all three of us, and possibly the others who just observe. The observed care-free interaction between man and beast brings smiles to others there.

RJ'S INTERVENTION

RJ was a psychotherapist with whom I had consulted several times prior to going into any facility, and of all the psychologists I felt I could identify the most, was with him. We had lost touch—as I had with reality at some point—when I had moved to Riverside Clinic, but my sisters rightly felt he could be of some assistance to me whilst in Butterfly Lodge. He agrees kindly to visit me at Butterfly Lodge, making appointments on a Saturday afternoon.

I am still very anxious and dysfunctional, but he gently speaks to me, setting up a contract between us. As I cannot—and will not—do things for myself, I have to set goals with him and then commit to him that I would meet them.

One of the first things is to get up every morning for schedule. I hate schedule, as after a month, it is so predictable that I could quote it in the same accent it is delivered to us in. Schedule was basically a breakdown discussion of the happenings and sessions for the day and as routine is important for people with mental stresses and illnesses, attending it is compulsory for all.

This occurs at 07h00 every morning, except for Sundays when it is a bit later, at 08h00.

In the first week following my return from Helen Joseph hospital, I manage to make it to schedule twice of my own accord. On the other occasions, I am coaxed by all and sundry to attend, but still delay partaking until it has been completed.

Dee tries every morning as she walks into my room, saying to me, "Craig, are you okay?"

"Yes, I am fine. I will be there now," but it's a lie.

This independent coaxing helps immensely, as now

I have made a commitment to her as well, and as such, feel an obligation to show up. Punishment for missing schedule was to do the dishes at lunch time, which was no mean feat as there were twenty of us at that stage. I hate washing dishes, and for a while, I hate schedule even more.

RJ has also contracted with me that I go shopping at Cresta Centre. The first weekend of the contract, I must go to the shops, spending the full three hours on my own, walking or alternatively sitting on my own in the shopping centre I have known for years. The anxiety is still debilitating, and I am fearful of being seen by anyone else I know outside of Butterfly Lodge. This is certainly no great achievement, but he thinks it is "one giant leap for this man, one small step for mankind".

The second week, I miss the shopping as I have not completed my diary, but this time, I feel the damage. For a change, I had wanted to go, as I am starting to feel better and more positive. My stubborn (or determined) side persists throughout this adventure, as I continue to never complete the diary.

For the third week post our contract, I manage to make it to all the schedules and receive applause for the effort of doing this without being coaxed (a small and very embarrassing endorsement). These small victories are noticed and welcomed by all the patients, as they recognise them for what they are: small steps on a very long and challenging walk through life.

THE BREAK THROUGH

The manager also has two particularly irritating and snappy Miniature Dobermans. I hate the yapping arrival of them, which coincides with the loud greetings of the sex addict at 06h30, so I decide to force myself to arise at 06h00 and 'beat the bell'. This, I believe, was one of my personal breakthroughs, as I came upon it of my own accord and stuck to it. Grabbing a cup of coffee, I greet anyone who is awake, move back outside into the garden, and sit and watch the sun rise.

Tom had left to go back to England to his family, and Heksie the happy dog took to greeting me instead. I slowly start taking over the role of primary attention giver. I had ignored all affection from people and animals for months by now, but decided to change how I am reacting by starting to embrace both man and beast as it were.

Beasts were about to take another role in my healing during art session. Starting to take part in the daily scheduled activities, I am cautious and avoid anything too emotional, limiting them to art initially.

Art is impersonal and I don't need to interact with people directly.

It is MY piece of paper, MY drawing, and MY space. Bearing in mind that I had not drawn ANYTHING in the two months since I had been admitted to Butterfly Lodge, I experience a moment where I surprise everyone. We must each select a picture from a collection of magazines and complete our artwork in any medium we choose.

Paging through a few magazines in the art room, I settle on a photograph of a herd of elephants and start putting pencil to paper. The grey swirls and shades on the white background start to take form and after two hours, it is complete.

At the end of the art session, we all display our work and tell the group why we have chosen that particular image. I have selected this one as the elephants are a powerful symbol of family unity. The destruction of my family unit was something that had initially destroyed me emotionally and then ultimately, the family unit that was left over from the original one, had saved me.

When elephants are in distress, they support, they don't abandon. They work as a family unit and as a broader group. If they need assistance from the herd outside of the direct maternal and paternal association with their calf, they will always assist.

They eat together, stay together, and will defend the individuals in the herd against all external threats. They are the epitome of the family unit.

Cautiously laying the drawing out on the floor in front of the other patients, I crack a broad grin as the other patients gasp in awe. They are as surprised as anyone could be, as the drawing of the small herd is a symbol of how quickly I have started to recover from the deep, dark place in which I had been stuck. It is an explosive awakening from a depressive, contemplative stupor and with the awakening comes a 'flurry' of activity. This is more like a grand entrance.

I suspect some patients were envious, not of the actual art work, but that someone had changed so quickly. There is no colour in the drawing yet, but the grey sketch has form and proportion and symbolism and hope. The water that my fronds and roots had tried so long to reach, have made an appearance in the picture and the elephants waded in contented. Colour could—and would, with time —follow in my life.

The drawing was a foundation for progress. It gave the others hope that there was an opportunity for them to possibly follow suit and be emancipated and freed from the mental anguish in which they still found themselves.

Knowing what I had created on paper and what it had meant to me and to them, makes me happy. Not elated, just happy. I just need it to stay as such. It was a huge leap forward, but the job at hand was now to keep the momentum going. I needed to enjoy the moment, breathe in the happiness, and feed off the other people's positivity that they had been so gracious in showering upon me.

Art and music once again became my gentle key to freedom.

One of the weekly activities offered was music and dance therapy. The class was run by two middle-aged men. They freely and comfortably exuded flouncing feminine traits and seemed to have a hankering for the old 'hippie' days as they clung to, or alternatively tried to revive that era with their loose-fitting tie-dyed trousers, blouson shirts, and bare feet with dirty soles. Long threads of hair clung on, trying desperately to survive on scalps where I suspect lush ponytails used to thrive. They had enthusiastic, gentle natures, and good intentions with a deep belief in the merits of their class and what it would deliver to our recovering group.

To avoid the embarrassment that any potential non-participants might cause in the depletion of presenter's egos, we are all to attend the classes. Those who don't want to partake in this form of therapy are forced to watch the other participants until the class is over. It is a matter of common courtesy to the presenters.

Being more akin to movement-to-music, I neither like the choice of music, nor the hip-swaying motions that are supposed to be prised from our rusted joints. I avoid these classes at all costs, because I feel as though I am being coerced to act like a bohemian hippie who is too darn sober to get into the mood. I refuse vehemently to prance around a room with arms swaying, pretending to be a flower, bird, or fantasy creature.

Emotions or personality traits that seemed to remain with me, or alternatively return first, were certainly those of stubbornness and embarrassment. And they came back strongly! On the odd occasion of being embarrassed, I am inclined to break out in a sweat and blush brightly and I refused to allow that to happen to me here. It was fine for some, but NOT for me, thank you very much.

Digging my heels in, I watch for a while from the peripheries as part of the reluctant audience, but then leave rapidly out of the room as the first opportunity presents itself to me. I am not the only one who feels this way, and Dee also times the 'exit stage left' with precision.

The work with RJ continues to improve, and I stick to our contract of participation what with going shopping, doing art, and starting to discuss things in therapy and in smaller informal social circles. Slowly, my voice starts to return.

Tom has returned home to England, so Dee and I strike up a friendship that is very gentle and caring. It is a very slow process where, for the outside observer, it must appear much like an adult coaxing a scolded, untrusting child out of a dark room or corner.

"Would you like to sit here, Craig?" Dee pats a place next to her on the couch. The other patients who are already crammed onto it, selflessly shuffle to the side just enough to create space for one additional skinny backside. The first couple of times, I turn her offer down with a, "No, thanks". The offers continue until eventually I agree to join watching sections of a film, departing quietly when I feel I have had enough. Progressively, after a few days, I manage to get through a full movie, slowly regaining my sense of humour, quietly coaxed by the comedy on screen.

During mealtimes, Dee reserves a chair at a table where we chat about general and then personal issues as I start voluntarily spending time with her. Being with her makes it so much easier to spend time with others. She, with her gentle soul, is my introduction back to humanity and life. Like a dolphin, she brought me back from the depths of a dark ocean and onto land where it was safer.

With time, I start talking to other people, becoming very involved with colouring in mandalas—an activity I thought futile just a few short weeks before. Simple sketches and colouring in of pre-drawn pictures eventually give way to detail. On weekends, I start spending time in the art room voluntarily, which is also the precursor to me listening to my music once again.

My music collection spanned forty years of variety and genre, but I had withdrawn from listening to any of it as every song and decade had an association with my wife. Even though I had not dated her at school, I knew who she was at the time and as such, had an association with the music even from those days. It was all too sad for me to remember the events linked to the songs, and for many long months, I tried to avoid being dragged back into that place in time.

In the art room, I start listening to the music again; starting with my heavier rock music I eventually move on to quieter, more emotional tunes. I am so afraid that an emotional awakening would be too hurtful and I want to avoid that possibility at all costs. And yet, I ultimately find out that it doesn't hurt anymore! Sharing my music with Dee, I manage to introduce her to many new classic artists from my generation. She is a lot younger than me, and has not been exposed to the classic songs that had shaped my life. The sharing builds a friendship and a bond of caring and kindness.

My self-induced wake-up call at 6 a.m. and a cup of coffee outside as the sun rises is followed by an all-too-brief bout of exercise. The many months of being sedentary have taken its toll and the sportsman I had once been has reduced to an emaciated, unfit male.

"Craig, if you want to move forward, there are two methods you can employ," says Kim at one of our visits.

"Here I am intentionally excluding the medication route. The one is to let the mind start and let it guide the body, and the other is to start with the body and it will kick-start the mind. Choose one."

"You have always been a sportsman and fitness enthusiast, so I think you should start with mild exercise."

For once, I listen.

Quivering arms agonisingly grind out between eight and ten push-ups, closely followed by spindly legs lifting a bony backside up with eight to ten free-standing squats. Finally, I end off with approximately ten sit-ups. This is all that my body can cope with. It has become just too weak for anything more than that! No more than ten minutes of very passive exercise. They are baby steps, but it is a start. My muscles are stiff the next day! And the next.

"Who's joining for the walk?" The regular question precedes a small procession of people to the front parking lot. It is time for me to respond to the question and join the group for the stroll through the neighbourhood, guided by one of the staff-members. I had previously chosen to avoid the walk; yet I now join in, always talking to Dee, and occasionally to the others in the group.

Shuffling upon unsteady legs, I point out the birdlife that has returned with the spring. As I have a moderate knowledge of the species in the area, I feel it might be of interest to the others and share openly.

The Crested Barbet sits in the tree boasting and claiming its territory with its cheerful shrill warbling and its raised multi-coloured crest. Arm pointed out at a dead tree stump with the hole chipped by sturdy beaks protected by the male and female Black-collared Barbets as they perch next to each other, harmonising with their happily co-ordinated calls.

"Go-waaay, go-waay!" the Grey Loerie warns the other species of the 'dangerous' human group that has wondered into their territory. Flocks of pigeons scatter as the small group makes its way down the sidewalks.

As we briskly stroll through the neighbourhood, I point out the Bougainvillea spectacularly clawing their way up the African garden walls claiming their colour from the sun's spectrum. They are particularly vibrant and prolific this spring, and the early rains have washed their dusty blooms clean. There had been no Bougainvillea in Jersey in the Channel Islands where Dee hailed from, and the floral beauty lifts her and the rest of us all up.

During these strolls, I notice that feeling was returning to my dead foot? I am able to lift it properly again. There is no more uncontrolled 'thud' as it used to slap down, but rather a controlled descent from heel to toe. Although I certainly can't run, I at least feel that I can do so once again. Any ambitions of attempting to run are stifled by a ridiculous vision of skinny me jogging uncomfortably down the road, loose fitting clothes flapping in the breeze and a 'minder' in hot pursuit trying to foil the attempted escape.

Dee has noticed my early morning exercise regime and after day two, decides to join me.

We are certainly no example to any sports fan as the process is painfully slow, but to us it is a start. We had both been good sports participants in our earlier years, and understand the need for health and fitness training. So, we try.

We are two very thin, tall people going through the motions. Trying, at least, we are way ahead of those opting to stay seated on the couch.

My eating regime starts to change dramatically. I no longer avoid meals, but play an active part in stuffing myself full of much-needed calories. Waiting for most people to finish their breakfast and move to the next class, I unobtrusively shuffle into the kitchen away from prying eyes. Standing at the kitchen table away from the dining room, I proceed to eat five bowls of cereal, never sitting down and ALWAYS facing the wall.

The process starts with the filling of two bowls with muesli and milk. This is quickly followed by another one with three blocks of hand-crushed Weet-Bix. Once this has been wolfed down, I gulp another two bowls of muesli mixed with sugar-covered Weet-Bix.

Filling the space that I had neglected and left empty for so many months, I start to regain my energy with massive servings of food. Will my body be able to go through the normal motions of processing what I have hurled at it? I am concerned that the calorie assault I have launched on my stomach and bowels will be a problem as I have starved myself for so long.

Lunch time is appropriately catered for, and limited to a generous platter for each person. If I'm still hungry, I will occasionally follow up with a couple of rusks dipped into a cup of coffee. Supper follows a similar pattern as my grateful and by-now accommodating stomach allows me to summarily clear my plate, and my weight starts picking up.

As the muscle had been unwillingly falling off my emaciated body for so many months, I had for so long been terrified of having my weight checked. I hate seeing the truth exposed to me in digital numbers at my feet and ribs protruding from my chest. The uncontrolled weight loss was both terrifying and hurtful and this truth would unsympathetically be exposed to all and sundry as they queued behind me awaiting their turn at the scale.

Yet, now my weight started to swing the other way. I notice how the scale changed its downward trend as the weight-drop stagnates and then slowly starts its way on an upward trend. 70...70.5...72...73 kilograms!

The relief is immense, as a few hundred grams are added at a time. Small corners are turned as good news awaits me each new day. People's positive, peering eyes notice along with me, too scared to believe what is happening in case of a relapse.

All depression-afflicted sufferers are warned and schooled by counsellors on noticing the signs of relapse that can so easily occur. Recovery can be temporary and yet, all will hope for a permanent positive change.

Relapse Prevention Plans (RPP) are often drawn up to help recognise the symptoms and then ward off the slide backwards by using special personalised techniques, good habits, and human support. As my depression was situational and I was confident I would not relapse, I felt no need to have an RPP. My RPP was to get back to all the old good habits I had followed prior to this emotional event. Eat well and regularly, exercise, drink lots of water, relax, and socialise with friends and family—who should be your support group, after all.

I was starting to gain clarity on my situation and the way out of it. Only THIS time, the clarity was not transitory. It seemed to remain firmly in place with seemingly no withdrawals or side-effects stealing my hope from my limp grasp.

___ ___ ___

Butterfly Lodge has a high turnover of staff. Dee had mentioned to me that the new psychologist allocated to her was very nice and easy to identify with. I was under the impression that I was still 'sectioned' and needed some clarity on the issue.

At this stage, I valued Dee's opinion and advice way beyond anyone else's in the facility. "You should speak to her, Craig," the simple recommendation flowed easily.

Once again, I listened to her as she had only good intentions for me and would always give me her honest, unbiased opinion. She was a highly qualified and intelligent woman who had seen this all-too-many sad times before.

I set up a meeting with Cheryl for the next day, and after a counselling session, I pose my big question. "Am I still sectioned and what control does management have over me at this stage?"

"I am not sure, Craig, but I tell you what I will do for you. In the management team discussion tomorrow, I will subtly ask the question and come back to you in a day or two. Is that okay?"

"Sure," is my hopeful response. A couple of days will certainly not be a problem. The rest of the day passes by in a blur of disinterest as the answer to the biggest question still hangs in the balance.

As promised, Cheryl calls me aside a few days later. Sitting down opposite her in the counselling room, I look across at her hopefully. No question is necessary as we are both acutely aware of what I want to hear… or do I want to hear it?

"Craig, you are not sectioned anymore, as long as you don't do anything stupid or irresponsible and keep taking your medicine, we can't keep you here any longer than the initial twelve weeks, as per the original contract."

I could have kissed her as the relief washed over me and a huge smile lights up my face. "Really?"

"Yes. Behave, and you are in the clear. The onus is on you now. Make good use of it."

"Good god, I will," flashes across my mind. I have hope once again!

No detail is needed on top of that, as I stride outside into the courtyard and, looking at Dee, gush the feedback to her, "I...AM...NOT...SECTIONED... ANYMORE!"

Hugging me, she beams "Oh, Craig, I am so happy for you!" As simple as that, yet it had REAL meaning!

Every hour of every day after that moment took on a whole different feel. Warm spring sunshine now strokes my shoulders. Cool nights ease my sleep. Stilted conversation is traded for casual, happy banter. Avoidance trades places with wilful participation and much-valued opinion for patients and useful feedback to counsellors as I slip back into life quicker than I had stepped out of it.

The Craig I had missed so much for so long, now became familiar as he re-took his place in my mind and body. The dirty, bearded, gaunt image that had for so long stared back questioningly at me from the mirrors and windows had now left, to be replaced by a trimmer, brighter, groomed, and functioning human being.

"AH... IT'S YOU... IT'S ME."
"I REMEMBER YOU."
"I MISSED YOU."
"WELCOME HOME."

"Hello, Craig. Pleased to meet you," Dee greets me again, intrigued with the newer old version she has just met. The Craig who was proud of what he had to show the world again.

"Pleased to meet you, too," the new old Craig returns the words.

NO, NOT ANOTHER CONTRACT

Lisa and Robert sit across from me, chatting away. A mid-week visit is so very welcome now.

"Dad, the management of Butterfly Lodge want you to stay for another three months. Mom is bringing the contract on Sunday."

Still protecting dad, "We know you want to leave and don't want to sign it, but are just letting you know so you are prepared."

Fortunately, it is MY choice once more.

"Thanks, Lisa, I appreciate the warning, but as you know, I am NEVER signing that form. I need to leave and move on with my life. I am ready for it."

I was more convinced than convincing, but the

decision was made. No one else had control over my life other than myself. I had won it back! What a sense of relief! There was NO chance I was going to let that happen. Twelve weeks was enough in one place, and twelve months of sadness had to be buried.

Friday afternoon prior to the Sunday visit, the managing director and the social worker call me into the office and raise the subject of the extended stay.

"Craig, we know you have made tremendous progress, but believe an additional three-month stay is necessary, and will do you good." Listening to them politely and having been forewarned by my children, when they were done, my retort is an empowered and blunt, "There is no way I am staying any longer. My mind is made up."

The vision of me incarcerated for another three months and over December when everyone else is on holiday, is untenable. No more needs to be said. Discussion over. I had turned the corner, figuratively speaking, and was determined to move on with my new life.

That Sunday, Jackie arrives an hour after my children and sits down as we greet her.

I notice the folded contract under her arm and smile to myself.

"No more. No fucking chance."

The four of us chat casually and naturally, as if the 'hiatus in hell' had never occurred. The realisation that I have made huge progress starts sinking in to them.

"Robert, let's get some tea and cold-drinks… Who wants what?"

We stroll off, leaving Lisa and Jackie behind in the garden, shortly returning with the drinks in hand. Handing the tea to Jackie, I notice that the contract has been set neatly aside. Its unnecessary detail shielded by a folded plastic sheath.

I do not need to see it. Don't waste your or my energy. The whole family now knows it is a done deal. The topic is not discussed. The contract would remain unsigned. Forever.

Later on, after Jackie had left, Lisa, Robert, and I remain seated at the table.

Lisa pipes up, "Dad, when you and Robert went to collect drinks, mom said, 'Gee, what a change!'" referring to my state of mind and attitude. I smile.

Yes, it was a change… a massive change. I was free to grow once again.

THE RETURN OF HAPPINESS

There was a time when it meant nothing
Then it changed
Love had loved
And love had left
Sadness had moved in
Whilst time shoved its way through
And beauty revealed itself
Soulfully
Slowly
I saw
Your eyes look at me

Staring and searing its beauty
Branded upon my heart
No day shared its sunshine as before
Summer lifted its head from its winter slumber
And the birds sang
Joy sprung
And released her happiness for all to see
The Jacaranda trees blinked their tears
From many purple lashes
As she rose,
Smiled and said
I am happy
Again

—*Craig Dawtrey*

THE LAST DAYS IN RECOVERY

During the last few weeks at the recovery unit, I slot into the required routines. As a privilege, I am given my cell phone back and once the battery is charged, start to communicate again with the outside world. I begin looking forward to life once again and set my goals. They are the same as the ones that came to me in the few windows that I had experienced when on the Mirtazapine, yet his time, I could carry them out with crystal-clear mind, clarity and confidence.

I am moved to another room where there are only two beds. The glass door and windows face the setting sun, so I can say goodbye to each day as time ticks towards my leaving. The opaque green sundial of sadness has been replaced by a clear clean glass of happiness. The normal living activities that had for so many months been impossible, become normal again—eating, drinking liquids, showering and shaving, and even going to the toilet as my insides return to a regular pattern.

No more derealisation, no more panic attacks, no more anxiety, pretty good sleep, and the previously absent smile I missed so much find its way back to my face! The human body is an amazingly resilient thing, and mine complies, allowing my healed mind to return to it and use it as it felt was fitting.

The last day at Butterfly Lodge ends with a 'graduation' session where all the other patients sit in a circle facing me and my children. In turn, each person says something personal and I reply with a "thank you" and a comment in return. The emotion displayed from each person—many accompanied by tears—is extremely heart-wrenching as I am surprised by the way I have affected the other patients in such positive ways. I was unaware of the influence we have had on each other's lives.

Dee is not able to make the party, as she has fallen ill that day.

Walking over to her room, I find her curled up on her bed. I hug and kiss her, and knowing how critical familiarity was in the healing process, tell her, "I will be visiting you every Sunday for visitor's day." Her family are overseas in Jersey and she received no visitors.

"Robert, Lisa… let's go!"

Packed suitcase in hand, I stride with my children to my car, climb in and drive confidently out of the driveway and on to my new rental home with my son and daughter. Out of Pine Avenue forever. I am not the homeless hobo left on the sidewalk.

--- --- ---

It's so damn cold as I shuffle in bare-footed as the aching path that scraped my soles from the car to the dojang is left behind.

I bow down... "Ahn young ha sim nee kah Kwan jung nim," (Good morning, grand master) is forced from my empty lungs like an old man. It has been a full year now and half a lifetime ago since I have trained with the legend. We have both aged, I see. The slightly greying Korean man in the same seat he was three hundred days ago, arises to reply with his greeting.

"Craig, you are too thin," he tactlessly continues. That is his way. Another culture from which no offense can and should be taken... He cares about me.

The still cold feet drag me across the mats to complete the greeting. This time, it is followed by a warm embrace. How do I tie the belt again? Cold, still uncoordinated fingers fumble as the knot is repeated for a second and third time... Oh yes, that's it!

The mutual bow completed, the stuttering stretching begins. Those damn hamstrings are pulling and crying out for me to stop! However, we will push, for that is the way of KWAN... the warrior's way. No complaining; listen to your body. Maintain respect. Fight for your wellness and fight for your life.

It is all a journey... one that has no finish. There is no perfection in this art. The shared, strained kicks and punches continue as the quieter bags sigh with relief... so much power has gone. Sweat drenches the uniform quicker now as the blue bruises start to appear from their red re-birth.

Compulsory order has given way to bad aim and form as the belt releases its proud tension around my thinner waist. Stop, catch your breath, and fix the belt.

"Con sa hom nee dha Kwan jung nim," (thank you, grand master).

--- --- ---

Many months later, and I am now settled into a new home with Robert and the two cats. Thirty-years-worth of memories had beenABC unceremoniously packed into boxes and along with unneeded furniture placed into storage, waiting for the appropriate time to be released from bondage.

Our home is adorned with every piece of family artwork and picture that has accompanied Lisa, Robert, and I from our family home. Natural progression determined that it would move along with us to the new house. Lisa has moved into a rental home and Robert and I have settled into the new space.

The furniture that came along from the previous house fits in perfectly. For some, it seems too much like the previous home, but I suspect that subconsciously, the similarity in earthy colours and wooden-framed windows has allowed me to gently ease into this new phase of life. I had been through enough trauma and need a slow introduction back into living.

After only twenty-four hours, it feels like home. It is our new 'bachelor-pad' with Robert, me, and the two male ginger cats, Tigger, and Fable.

For a full year, I had avoided sifting through the

photographs, even though Jackie had suggested that we meet at the storage and "sort things out". My response at that stage had been a simple, "I can't do that. It is too cold."

A few months later, I singularly decide I will remove boxes in stages, bringing them home to be sorted out. I would keep what I feel is needed, and what I have an important emotional attachment to. Once sorted out, I take the remnants of the photograph album and place it back in the box and return it to storage for her to keep what she wanted. The pictures had captured places in time, yet, they have lost all significance.

The one person I was supposed to reminisce with over time, had moved on, and the photographs have become merely images on paper. For me, they have no meaning of any significance anymore. It was someone else's life that I had featured in. I had played a part in their scripted story, and once I had served my purpose, had been discarded in the box along with the photographs.

Our children's births, their first plays and days at school. Sports-events and birthday-parties. "Keep this one... She can have that one."

Once again, a fast-forwarding of our lives speeds past in static images. Extended intimate family holidays and then the large family ones with both sides of the family—over twenty people congregated for a moment in time. These will be no more.

"Two copies of this one, so we can each keep a copy."

At what stage had the deception started? A year

ago? Ten years ago? Before the last anniversary? After a business trip? All is sadly questioned and the doubt extends back as far as I can think.

"She's in this one, so she can keep it." Into the box.

I glance down at the pile of photographs that have been dumped in the box-of-no-return and think about how this has become a graphic representation of what had happened to our lives. And some have already faded.

Whilst searching for my scuba diving equipment, I come across a large plastic bag in one of the cupboards in a spare room. Opening it in haste, I am surprised to find it stuffed full of at least ten pairs of ladies' shoes… their mouths still agape. It is a stark reminder of how quickly my life had changed and Jackie had moved out of our house and our family life. They had been carelessly discarded, or alternatively, conveniently left behind with her previous life. I donate the shoes to a car-guard at a shopping centre.

OUR OCEAN BOND

Silent movies from our youth
And sepia images
Stir our memories
As they sting our sunburnt skin with smiles and giggles
Returning us to our roots
And gently drawing the heart-felt love out of our albums
And
Then

Returning to the ocean
We find peace in knowing
That some things have not changed
Our memories
And family's spirit
Lean back to glance up
And request from the sun
As it descends
To scratch silver and gold from the blue sky
And bathe us again
In joy and comfort
And let us know
All is still good
Until tomorrow's tide strokes the sand and
Coats us again with a salty
New happy memory

—*Craig Dawtrey*

THE BEGINNING

CONCLUSION

ON MEDICATION AND PSYCHIATRIC DRUGS

Doctors had put me on the following medication groups during the twelve-month experiment;

- Benzodiazepines
- Selective Serotonin Reuptake inhibitors (SSRIs)
- Serotonin and Norepinephrine Reuptake Inhibitors (SNRI's)
- Beta Blockers

And as individual drugs;

- Serdep (Zoloft)
- Serlife (Zoloft) later on
- Dormicum
- Dormonoct
- Remeron

- Mirtazepine
- Seroquel
- Dopaquel
- Stilnox (Imovane)
- Pur Bloka (Propranolol)
- Fluoxetine (Prozac)
- Ativan
- Alzam

Medical staff, in my opinion, are far too enthusiastic to prescribe pills to 'fix' things, and at one stage, had me poly-drugged and on five of the above-mentioned drugs AT THE SAME TIME! I also believe that the worsening of the depression was possibly anti-depressant induced.

These medicines fixed nothing. They merely masked emotions and symptoms in the hope that the problem could be ironed over. I believe whole-heartedly that the 'mental illness' illustrated in this account of my year was Iatrogenic (an Iatrogenic illness is caused by medication or physician). My sadness or decline or depression was a reaction to a shock in my life that was not expected. In other words, it was situational.

Having now been off all medication for several years, and having suffered no side–effects or withdrawals after this last drug, I am moved to conclude that I don't know if the Fluoxetine had any role to play in my healing. It was the only medication that I had no noticeable side-effects on, other than a not–so-good short-term memory. At the same time, I felt absolutely no difference or withdrawals whilst weaning myself off the medication or at any stage after the last dose. I made the decision to go off all medication; yet, not all patients feel the same way. Some fear what the possible consequences might be.

Lauren Slater, in her book, *The Drugs That Changed our Minds*, tells of her own experience and decision; *"It's reasonable to ask why, other than out of a deference to authority, I myself didn't stop when the prescription didn't help me at all. I can only say that after a while, although the drug offered no relief, I worried that if I went off it, I'd get even worse."*

I am led to understand that psychotropic drugs have helped many people; yet, I have seen how the side-effects and withdrawals have destroyed lives as much, if not more.

Lauren Slater continues;

"In the end Psychiatry has sickened me even as it has saved me... Psychiatry has yet to find a drug that does not exact a physical price. Everything in the psychopharmacological arsenal gives and takes. Sometimes the price is uncertainty itself, because no-one knows what chronic use of any of these medicines really does to the brain of people who have been chronically exposed to Imipramine, the MAOI's, fluoxetine or chlorpromazine, in part because few long-term users give their brain to science upon their death, preferring to go to the grave intact."

In my personal case, I believe it was a very bad decision having agreed to take medication prescribed by doctors (one general practitioner and three psychiatrists in total). If we feel we need a medical diagnosis, then my case of sadness or depression was situational, and I doubt the wisdom of being prescribed medication so quickly.

I should possibly have taken another approach. None of these doctors seemed to listen to my complaints about the side-effects and none of them seemed to have a clue as how to wean me off. Instead, one of the psychiatrists said I had "Borderline Personality Disorder" due to the symptoms (read side-effects) I had been displaying, in addition to the other diagnoses described at Helen Joseph Hospital. I slowly removed myself from the drug regime whilst listening to my body, and responding to the feelings and sensations I was continuously very aware of.

I should instead have merely taken time off and allowed the emotion to filter through me, and in the process, wash my hurt soul clean. The side-effects and withdrawal symptoms were debilitating and did me no favours whatsoever. They made me at best seem incapable and weak, and at worst, nearly killed me by either destroying my body and or mind.

I am unfortunately a massive cynic of the whole psychiatric fraternity because of my having experienced it first-hand from the 'other' side. Simply put, it took away almost a year of my life, and in the process, nearly took away my life completely. My opinion is that it is an incomplete science at best; at worst, its application by many psychiatrists is merely advanced quackery. The doctor guesses what the patient should be prescribed based on what he or she is telling the doctor, and the doctor believes all the flowery health speak the pharmaceutical companies and representatives are spewing out to them.

This process of diagnosis is taken from the 'Diagnostic and Statistical Manual of Mental Disorders' (DSM) and is published by the 'American Psychiatric Association' (APA).

It is evident that more and more professionals in the field are beginning to question the status quo with regards to antidepressants and psychiatric medications, as the following quotes show;

"...when people come off antidepressants and then experience withdrawal, the doctor looks at the The National Institute for Health and Care Excellence (NICE) guidelines and concludes it can't be withdrawal. Patients are regularly having their withdrawal reaction either denied, ignored or, most concerningly, misdiagnosed as a relapse of their condition, at which point the drugs are reinstated".

And,

"Researchers looked at 23 studies over 20 years and found that 56% of all patients on antidepressants suffer withdrawal symptoms, of which 46% said their symptoms were severe".

—Dr. James Davies, co-author and a reader in medical anthropology and mental health at the University of Roehampton

"...shows that official documents and the psychiatric profession have not taken this issue seriously, not put enough effort into researching it and not wanted to face up to the problems that these drugs cause". "We're giving people these drugs for years on end and we haven't bothered to work out what happens to them, how that affects the body, and what happens when people stop them. That seems just outrageous, a terrible situation."

—Dr. Joanna Moncrieff, a psychiatrist and leading critic of the overuse of antidepressants

"We want NICE to acknowledge that antidepressant withdrawal is more common, long-lasting and severe than current guidelines state, and to oblige doctors to warn patients."

—Professor John Read, psychologist

"The antidepressants are an effective, evidence-based treatment which were a life-saver to many people. But not enough research has been done into what happens when you stop taking them...for many people the withdrawal effects can be severe, particularly when antidepressants are stopped abruptly." She adds, "Many, would not start taking them if they knew the battle they might have getting off them, the data is now there, and both doctors and patients need to be cautious about starting antidepressants in the first place."

—Professor Wendy Bur

It is a lottery where they sometimes get it right, but I believe mostly, get it wrong. Too many people are walking this earth medicated for symptoms that are side-effects of the drugs or withdrawal symptoms from them going off other drugs that have been prescribed by the same or another psychiatrist. Patients and survivors of these drugs need to be listened to more often in order for the psychiatrists and pharmaceutical companies to learn more about their own trade.

For those who have loved ones still going through what I have survived and those that are living with the affliction and bad medicine:

WHAT WE WISH FAMILY AND FRIENDS KNEW ABOUT PSYCHIATRIC MEDICATION WITHDRAWAL

"If we had been diagnosed with cancer, our family and friends would know that we are sick. They'd make us casseroles, take us to our chemo appointments, and call us to see how we are doing. After all, cancer is a serious matter. They would be concerned. But family and friends have very little knowledge about psychiatric medication withdrawal so they don't know just how serious it is.

"We trusted our doctors and took a pill, as prescribed and it damaged one of the two main "circuit boards" that regulate our brains. We have damaged GABA receptors, which means our bodies and minds don't have the ability to slow/calm down. We suffer from

chemical brain damage that can take a long time (sometimes years) to heal. Many of us have severe physical symptoms: painful joints, bones, muscles teeth, eyes, mouth, etc. Our skin burns. It feels as if we have bugs crawling under our skin, or that bees are stinging us. Our muscles twitch and spasm. Our legs are weak and our balance is off, walking is difficult. But some of us do walk, and walk, and walk, as we are suffering from akathisia, a movement disorder that causes an inner ear restlessness and a compelling need to be in constant motion.

"We have painful and frightening pressure in our heads, making it feel as if the world is sloshing around us. Many of us are bedridden for months at a time, unable to take care of the most basic of human needs. We can't think properly, and our memory is impaired. There are countless other physical symptoms that we may have as this is not an extensive list. What we want our friends and family to know is that we are sick and in pain. It's hard to manage our lives. Many of us are unable to work or to function in our roles and duties as parent. On top of being physically sick, we have mental symptoms as well.

"Without a functioning GABA system to calm the fight/flight/freeze response of our brains, we live in a state of fear, anxiety, paranoia, or terror. We may have depersonalisation or derealisation. Frequent panic attacks are common. In 'psychiatric medication withdrawal', we lose the ability to feel positive emotions. Love, happiness and joy are not within our reach. We slog through our days feeling zombie-like

doom and gloom. Intrusive and looping thoughts are common. We have very little control of our minds. Visual, auditory, and olfactory hallucinations are not uncommon. We wish that our friends and family understood how frightening it is to lose the ability to think rationally and to no longer feel as if you are the same person you were before psychiatric medication' withdrawal. It is hard to live in the altered reality that the withdrawal can create.

"We want friends and family to know that we are scared and oftentimes feeling hopeless. We need a great deal of reassurance. When we get scared that we will never get well, that we will never be ourselves again, we want you to remind us that we are healing. We know that we tax your patience, and feel bad about being so needy. But we hope that you can hang in there with us as we do the hard work of holding on and surviving. We want you to take care of yourself so that you have the energy to take care of us too when we need your help. Please don't burn out! It's okay to take time away from us to refresh and recharge.

"We know that the only cure for psychiatric medication withdrawal is time, so your suggestions to "Go see a doctor" or "Get back on your meds," or "Up your dose", doesn't help us. See, what you don't know is that the medical community understands very little about the damage these drugs cause. We've learnt from thousands of others who have lived through withdrawal. There are no meds for withdrawal, nor should anyone be on a psychiatric medication for more than a few days. Please trust

that we have educated ourselves about the healing process from psychiatric medications.

"We want our friends and family to know that psychiatric medication withdrawal will come to an end one day, (even if we don't believe that ourselves). Our brains and our bodies will heal. We will start new chapters in our lives. We want everyone that we love to go the distance with us and to celebrate the dawning of the new day when we are recovered. Until then we just need you to listen to us, to be there for us. We don't need you to try and fix us, we know that you can't."

—By Jennifer Leigh as posted on *Friends in Recovery from Benzodiazepines*, a closed group on Facebook

PSYCHIATRIC MEDICATION RECOVERY TIPS

1. Recovery from being an accidental addict to psychiatric medication (Xanax, Klonopin, Ativan) is serious business. It takes time for the central nervous system to heal and for neurotransmitters to stop being sensitive. None of us had the faintest idea that this kind of situation lay in front of us. So, we are dealing with shock at what has happened as well as the real physical and mental/emotional symptoms of withdrawal.

2. Recovery is not linear, as it is with other illnesses or injuries. If we cut our hands, we can actually

see the cut heal and the pain diminish over time. In psychiatric medication' withdrawal we can be well one day and very sick the next. This is normal and we have to look at our healing differently.

3. Recovery is an individual thing, and it is difficult to predict how quickly symptoms will stop for good. People expect to be completely better after a certain period of time, and often get discouraged and depressed when they feel this time has passed and they are not completely better. Most patient support programs tell clients to anticipate 6 months to a year for recovery after a taper has ended. But some people feel better a few months after they stop taking psychiatric medications. For others it takes more than a year to feel completely better. Try not to be obsessed with how long it will take, because every day you stay off psychiatric medication's, your body is healing at its own rate. If you do not follow this schedule, it does not mean there is something wrong or you are not healing. Even if you are feeling ill in some respects, other symptoms may disappear. Even people in difficult tapers see improvements in symptoms very early on. So, don't let these time frames scare you. The way you feel at one month will not be how you will be feeling after three months or at six months.

4. It is very typical to have setbacks at different points of time (these times can vary). These

setbacks can be so intense that people feel their healing hasn't happened at all; they feel they have been taken right back to the beginning. Setbacks, if they occur, are a normal part of recovery.

5. When people are in recovery, they have a lot of fears. One is that they will never get better. Another is that their symptoms are really what they are like – perhaps what they have always been like. Both fears are stimulated by psychiatric medication withdrawal, just as insomnia is a physical component.

6. There is no way around psychiatric medication withdrawal and recovery– you must go through it. People try all sorts of measures to make the pain stop, but nothing can shortcut the process. Our body and brain have their own agenda for healing, and it will take place if you simply accept it.

7. When you are having a bad spell, healing is still going on. People typically find that after a bad spell, symptoms improve and often go away for ever. Try to remember this when times are hard.

8. There is no magic cure for recovery, but you can help yourself by comforting and reassuring yourself as much as possible. Read assuring information, stay away from stress, ask your partner, family, and others for reassurance, and

go back to the things you did at the beginning if you are experiencing tough symptoms.

9. When we start to feel better, it is very typical to try and do too much. We are grateful to be alive and we have energy for the first time in weeks or months. But this can be a dangerous time. When we do too much and take on too much too early, it re-sensitises the nervous system. It doesn't prevent healing in the long term, but it can make us feel discouraged. So, try and pace yourself, even if you are feeling good.

10. You do need to respect your body during recovery, although you don't need to make drastic changes in your lifestyle. Exercise, in any form, is critical – even if you can only walk around the house or to the end of the block. Eating well and avoiding stimulants is crucial. Regular high-protein snacks can help with the shakes and feelings of weakness we have during withdrawal and recovery.

11. Recovery is all about acceptance, but this does not mean passive acceptance. Set small goals for yourself that are achievable. Try to keep exercise happening. Work at your recovery even if that means accepting you are sick – for now. You wouldn't be hard on yourself if you were in a traffic accident and had injuries; you would work at rehab. Try to take the same attitude and approach to psychiatric medication withdrawal.

ON MARRIAGE AND COMMUNICATION

Ah
I see you are here again!
You always seem to sneak in
Unannounced and uninvited
You don't seem to have aged at all
The flecks in your hair still cling to yesterday
As your eyes do sell me promises so long ago betrayed
What are you doing here?
Bringing mementos from our children
And a home you so long ago abandoned
The key of permission that was withdrawn by me
You keep re-cutting
As the way you cut my heart open
And left me to bleed
My home is no more an open one to you
And my mind's welcome
I banished you from long ago
When you were within reach then
Loneliness stole my sleep
Yet now when slumber owns me
I will not touch you
So once again
How do you permeate my sleep
And darken my night?

—Craig Dawtrey

Marriage is intended for a lifetime, and we state this in front of many people when we start out on this journey. Yet, I now understand that obstacles will get in the way that may seem insurmountable and, in many cases, they might be so. However, my request is this: when these obstacles cross your path and you are not sure whether you can overcome them, then TALK UP!

Talk up, and soon! Tell your partner what the problem is and how it is affecting you and by extension, your marriage. At the very least, when and if the marriage still fails, you can confidently state "I tried". Your conscience will be clear.

Using statements after the fact like, "Something had to change", is worth nothing unless that person who is involved with you knows what THAT 'something' is. He, or she, cannot work on 'something'. Verbalize what is bothering you, and make it damn clear. In other words, give the spouse the chance to fix it. If they don't make the effort to change themselves or what they are doing 'wrong', then it is possibly time to move on.

Speak to your spouse first. It is pointless confiding in someone outside of the marriage until you have broached the subject with your spouse. He or she cannot hear this discussion if they are not involved in it.

Additionally, the person you confide in might have another agenda. They might actually be in love with you or hate your spouse. If either of these is the case, then they will NEVER be objective in their opinion and the advice will be skewed toward what they would like to see happen with your relationship. The person 'helping you through the process' might very well be steering you, just like the Titanic, directly at your marital ice-berg and their solution is their rescue-boat conveniently positioned where the marriage sinks. NOT everyone has honest intentions. Either way, this break-up, if it happens, is GOING to hurt someone. No one comes out of this unscathed.

As I look down at my left hand and notice the slightly faded and wrinkled loop around my wedding finger, I see a subtle reminder of the twenty-seven years of which it was covered by a gold band. A gold band that signified a connection, a commitment, and a bond. A gold band that, although scuffed with reminders of hardships and life experiences, still shone brightly for a few months as it waited, hoping for a positive ending.

This bond is now broken, yet the wrinkled patch that remains on that finger functions as a reminder of the tenuous link that remains between us. One that is tethered forever by our children and fading memories. I don't know if the wrinkled faded loop will ever smooth out, and along with that, the last remnants of the relationship that ended in such pain and sadness will disappear. As they say, 'only time will tell'.

I suspect that I will forever be saddened by the fact that what has happened has resulted in the unenviable fact that our children, though young adults, now come from a broken home and a once large, extended family that is now fractured with contact fading daily.

ON LIVING AND LIFE

I can never give you guarantees
I can never give you life
A view from above is a dream I long to lift you to
To snatch a brief glimpse of
If I have the gift of permission
From your light
From your beautiful dreams that I cannot see
May I be showered with satisfying your aspirations
Filtered through from your veil
And then trickled down to mine
Your hopes that may have been
Snatched and faded by others
Stolen and jaded by souls that
Are thieves of ambition and hope
May I gift to you the happy answers once again
Only this time in the wrappings you wished for
And once freed in your own time
May they bring you the unseen
And unspoken dreams you held hidden from yourself
And may they be good
Always

—Craig Dawtrey

Over a period of time, I have weaned myself off all the psychiatric medication I had been prescribed, and suffer no withdrawals or side-effects. I did this very carefully and slowly and listened to my body and what it was telling me, and NOT what the psychiatrists said. I believe if I had told them what my plans were, they would have kept me on medication, which I am not prepared to endure again. I am not advocating for all patients to go off medication as I am not medically qualified to give this advice. I AM however fully qualified by my experience to be able to say that it was a horrific experience on that medication as much as it was going off cold turkey at the recovery facility. There are many groups online that can be consulted for direction and these are all people going through what I did.

I am happy once again in that I now think clearly, and am full of the energy I had before being medicated. I have regained all the muscle mass (twenty-four kilograms) I had lost, thanks to hard exercise and eating healthily.

There are occasions where I doubt my short-term memory as it occasionally fails me, and I wonder if that is as a result of the chemical torture my brain endured.

I am also aware that a human needs to feel emotion and experience all of them to be a whole person. Having psychotropic drugs dull every emotion did me no favours, and I am happy to be able once again to laugh, cry, feel anger, and agitation without it being overbearing. Anxiety is moderate to non-existent, and I fear very little as I know I have hit the bottom and have stared death in the face and beaten it off, hopefully for many years to come.

Relationships with friends and family have been rekindled and stabilised to the point where I feel like a 'normal' person once again. I fill a functioning contribution to society in that I can once again read and write and support my family and community. I am fortunate enough to once again be able to support myself financially through work, and have regained my independence in order to make my own decisions on my future.

I still have days where I sit back and think quietly to myself, or then again on occasion vocalise it aloud to people close to me, "What the fuck happened?"

Everything I feared in terms of my loss have come to pass, with the loss of my marriage, her extended family, my previously tight family unit of four, having left her family business, and on occasion, having the 'dinner for one'.

EVERYTHING HAS CHANGED, contrary to her assurances; yet, I am ready for it now. Time has assisted in the healing and my 'new normality' is very acceptable and at times, quite wonderful. I still have my delightful son living with me in our new home and although my daughter lives in her own home near to me, I have her beautiful, funny-minded support and love. They are my rock and reason for living and THAT was what got me through this very challenging episode in my AND their lives. I am fortunate to have them.

Printed in Great Britain
by Amazon